COUNTER-HISTORY OF THE PRESENT

Gabriel Rockhill

COUNTER-HISTORY
of the Present

*Untimely Interrogations
into Globalization,
Technology, Democracy*

Duke University Press | Durham and London | 2017

© 2017 Gabriel Rockhill
All rights reserved

Typeset in Warnock Pro by Westchester Publishing Services

Originally published in French: *Contre-histoire du temps présent: Interrogations intempestives sur la mondialisation, la technologie, la démocratie*. Paris: CNRS Éditions, 2017.

Library of Congress Cataloging-in-Publication Data
Names: Rockhill, Gabriel, author.
Title: Counter-history of the present : untimely interrogations into globalization, technology, democracy / Gabriel Rockhill.
Description: Durham : Duke University Press, 2017. |
Includes bibliographical references and index.
Identifiers: LCCN 2016053070 (print) | LCCN 2016058882 (ebook)
ISBN 9780822369646 (hardcover)
ISBN 9780822369769 (pbk.)
ISBN 9780822372882 (e-book)
Subjects: LCSH: Philosophy, Modern. | Globalization—Philosophy. | Technology—Philosophy. | Democracy—Philosophy.
Classification: LCC B791.R635 2017 (print) | LCC B791 (ebook) |
DDC 909.83—dc23
LC record available at https://lccn.loc.gov/2016053070

Cover art: Alex Chinneck's sculpture *Take my lightning but don't steal my thunder*. Photo by Chris Tubbs Photography.

to my children
to children
and to the composition
of rich and profound
counter-histories,
without end

Nothing appears more surprizing to those, who consider human affairs with a philosophical eye, than the easiness with which the many are governed by the few; and the implicit submission, with which men resign their own sentiments and passions to those of their rulers. When we enquire by what means this wonder is effected, we shall find, that, as FORCE is always on the side of the governed, the governors have nothing to support them but opinion. It is therefore, on opinion only that government is founded; and this maxim extends to the most despotic and most military governments, as well as to the most free and most popular.

—DAVID HUME

CONTENTS

xi ACKNOWLEDGMENTS

1 INTRODUCTION
Toward a Counter-History of the Present

11 CHAPTER 1
A Specter Is Haunting Globalization

33 CHAPTER 2
Are We Really Living in a Technological Era?

51 CHAPTER 3
What Is the Use of Democracy?
Urgency of an Inappropriate Question

103 AFTERWORD
Taking Charge of the Meanings and Directions of History

109 NOTES

133 BIBLIOGRAPHY

143 INDEX

ACKNOWLEDGMENTS

This book has been nurtured by many dialogues and discussions with friends and colleagues. It would be impossible to make an exhaustive list here, but I would particularly like to thank Avi Alpert, Roei Amit, Alice Canabate, Eric Carlson, Pierre-Antoine Chardel, Andrès Claro, Andrew Feenberg, Marie Goupy, Emily Rockhill, Julian Sempill, Ádám Takács, Yannik Thiem, and all of the participants in the Critical Theory Workshop/Atelier de Théorie Critique 2014. I would also like to express my gratitude to the activist circles in Philadelphia and the surrounding area (including at Graterford Prison).

I wish to thank as well all of the organizations and institutions that invited me to present some of the research that led to this book: LASCO—Monde Contemporain (Université Paris Descartes), Penn Humanities Forum (University of Pennsylvania), Eszterhazy Karoly College (Eger, Hungary), Atelier—Centre Franco-hongrois en Sciences Sociales, Eötvös Loránd University (Budapest, Hungary), American Comparative Literature Association, New York University in France, and Tekst, Bilde, Lyd, Rom, or TBLR (Norway). I am also grateful to Villanova University, and in particular to the Office of Research and Sponsored Projects and the Publications Board for the grants that facilitated the completion of this work. Previous versions of two chapters were published in collections, whose editors and publishers I would like to thank: "Un spectre hante le concept de mondialisation," in *Technologies de contrôle dans la mondialisation: Enjeux politiques, éthiques et esthétiques*, ed. Pierre-Antoine Chardel and Gabriel Rockhill, 81–105 (Paris: Éditions Kimé, 2009), and "Contre-histoire de la technologie: Vers une écologie des pratiques technologiques," in *Écologies sociales: Le Souci du commun*, ed. Pierre-Antoine

Chardel and Bernard Reber (Lyon: Éditions Parangon, series "Situations & Critiques," 2014). The first article was translated into English by Emily Rockhill as "A Specter Is Haunting Globalization," and it appeared in *Cognitive Architecture: From Bio-politics to Noo-politics*, ed. Deborah Hauptmann and Warren Neidich, 470–87 (Rotterdam: 010 Publishers, 2010). Unless otherwise indicated, all translations are my own.

I would like to express my gratitude to Claire Thierry and Alice Canabate for their diligent proofreading of the original manuscript in French and their valuable editorial advice regarding *Contre-histoire du temps présent: Interrogations intempestives sur la mondialisation, la technologie, la démocratie* (Paris: CNRS Éditions, 2017). I am grateful as well to Emily Rockhill and John V. Garner, who prepared diligent translations of chapter 1 and chapters 2 and 3 respectively, and who allowed me to work very closely with them in establishing the final English versions. Finally, I would like to thank the editorial staff at Duke University Press, and particularly Courtney Berger, for immediately supporting this project and helping me see it through to completion.

INTRODUCTION

# Toward a Counter-History of the Present

Definierbar ist nur das, was keine Geschichte hat.
—Friedrich Nietzsche

We hear from nearly all sides that we are living in a global era in which a technico-economic network increasingly joins together the four corners of the globe, and democracy imposes itself as the necessary condition for political life. Rapid technological and economic development would seem, according to certain people, to go hand in hand with the triumph of democracy, as if they mutually reinforced one another. Some have even come to proclaim the end of history, thereby striving to surreptitiously recuperate, by perverting its fundamental meaning, a certain Marxian discourse. Yet it is not at all necessary to go to such lengths in order to be caught within the same historico-political imaginary.[1] Independently of ideological orientations, historical common sense induces us to conceive of our age as one in which the world has become truly global, new technologies have been veritable game-changers, and the idea of democracy reigns supreme.

However, this image of a global age, as advanced as it is civilized, is far from going without saying. Is it legitimate, for instance, to speak of globalization while one-sixth of the world's population is living in slums—which are sometimes cut off from national and international modes of governance, as well as from many forms of networked communication—and global wealth is increasingly concentrated in the hands of an infinitesimal minority of elites?[2] Is it true that we live in a new era of technological development, even though less than half of the global population (43.4 percent) has regular Internet access?[3] Can one honestly speak of a consensus on democracy when many states that consider themselves democratic have been openly hostile to democratic politics around the world (the American government, which prides itself on being the global showcase for democracy, has endeavored to overthrow more than fifty foreign governments, the majority of which had been democratically elected)?[4] From this point of view, such an image of the present not only seems dubious, but can also be dangerous. What is more, the close ties that it maintains with the dominant political imaginary recall colonial historiography in more ways than one.

This is not to suggest in the least, of course, that this historico-political imaginary is absolutely hegemonic and ubiquitous, nor is it to insinuate that there are no forces that have been actively resisting it. On the contrary, it is but one imaginary among others, although it is arguable that it has sought to forcefully impose itself as the only option, striving to definitively capture and frame our common understanding of the contemporary world. An expansive, cross-disciplinary, and international constellation of critical work has, in various ways and from motley vantage points, highlighted some of its important failings and distortions. Moreover, political praxis, in a significant number of different settings, has cultivated—with remarkable success in certain instances—alternative practices of collective world making, rival technological ecologies, and modes of governance more worthy of the reputation of the name *democracy*.

One of the objectives of this book is to contribute to these movements and this constellation of radical critique, which ultimately aim at reconfiguring the contemporary process of collectively forging a cosmos. By undertaking an investigation that would need to be qualified as untimely, it lodges a deep and systematic challenge to this widespread vision of the present. In order to do so, it focuses on the intertwining relationship between three key concepts: globalization, technology, democracy. This ensures it a precise angle of analysis, especially because they form a relatively coherent ensemble.[5] Yet this approach should not suggest that such notions sum up, on their own, the predominant historico-political imaginary of our conjuncture. The concepts of terrorism, security, the international community, productivity, or austerity—to cite but a few examples—are equally important and deserve to be examined in turn. Fundamentally, what I am interested in is the construction, circulation, and reception of a certain image of the present, and the concepts chosen constitute only three points of entry among others.

The second objective of this book is to forge theoretical tools allowing us to approach the problematic of contemporary reality from a completely different perspective. The counter-history undertaken here does not consist in proposing an alternative history from the same basic phenomena or from the same historical logic or order. It is much rather a question of breaking with the epochal thinking of the dominant historical imaginary by demonstrating that it is impossible to reduce history to its sole chronological dimension, since there is always a geography of the present and a variable experience of "contemporary reality" depending on social strata and points of view. The most prevalent historical imaginary tends to blur or obscure such differences by imposing a single hegemonic image of time on the totality of the world, which has considerable political, social, cultural, ethical, psychological, and economic consequences.

A counter-history calls into question the very idea of a sole and unique present that would everywhere be the same, and that one could define with a single concept or set of uniform defining characteristics.[6] It does not, therefore, propose an opposite history of contemporary reality that would quite simply reverse a conventional conception of our conjuncture in order to show the inverse. It does not mobilize dialectical machinery, and it does not play a simple game of antagonism or reversal. The argument in this book is not that we need to simply invert our current understanding of the world in order to reveal the truth, nor is it that all of the phenomena that have been foregrounded by the dominant imaginary do not exist in the least or are simple illusions. In *countering* a particular schematization of contemporary reality, it specifically *counters* the historical order that underpins it. This double counter-history does not limit itself, therefore, to calling into question alleged historical positivities—so-called incontestable givens—but it strives to modify the very logic that has produced them. This implies diligent and delicate work on the ways in which history has been historically constituted as a practice that frequently relies on a unidimensional conception of space and privileges a very specific form of chronology (often Eurocentric and anthropocentric). Counter-history counters history, then, in the precise sense that it mounts a relentless struggle against its own proper historicity, which is to say against the historical constitution of the unquestioned givens of certain ways of doing history. In other words, instead of simply proposing another history, counter-history aims at changing the very meaning—and direction—of history and narrative (*le sens même de l'histoire*), in all senses of these terms, and at thereby modifying the field of possibilities.

Counter-history seeks to retool historical methodology in such a way that history itself becomes a multidimensional phenomenon. This means that its temporal dimension is thought in relationship to both its spatial and social dimensions. Rather than history operating in terms of a largely linear, chronological development, it is geographically and socially distributed in various ways. Instead of proposing, then, one more master concept—such as postmodernism, the digital age, the era of empire—to purportedly capture the unique nature of the present, a counter-history begins by deconstructing the very idea of "the present" (which itself is most often defined ethnocentrically, thereby projecting "our present" onto the rest of the world). In this regard, as we shall see, a counter-history is necessarily a counter-geography and a counter-sociology.

The notion of a phase proves itself to be particularly important to this project. Unlike an epoch, an age, or a historical time period, a phase is always distributed in a precise manner across time as well as in space and in society. It develops via historical metastases, which is to say variable rate transformations that are unequally spread over social space-time. This is one of the starting points for outlining the rudiments of an alternative logic of history that is capable of sketching, from specific sociohistorical bracing points, the broad lines of a historical conjuncture. By conjuncture, we must not understand a homogeneous space-time or an epoch susceptible to being enclosed within a single container concept, if it be the notion of globalization, that of the ascendency of new technologies, or that of the triumph of democracy. A conjuncture is a specific meeting point between the three dimensions of chronology, geography, and sociality. If a conjuncture can be mapped, at least up to a certain point, this is not because there is some spirit of the times by which history ends up subjecting itself to the power of the concept. It is because it is possible to propose topological captures, meaning fallibilist cartographies anchored in particular perspectives. For the act of calling into question a widespread image of the present and the historical order on which it depends is not equivalent to giving up on the challenge of thinking the contemporary. On the contrary, it is an attempt to clear an untimely path toward a historical order allowing us to propose a completely different organization of our conjuncture. It is very important to emphasize in this regard that the topological captures proposed below obviously do not claim to lay hold, once and for all, of the true nature of our time. These are instead interventions in specific force fields that are consciously part of a social epistemology. Indeed, what we call historical truth is actually an issue at stake in social struggles, and it would be naive to believe that there is a level playing field in this area (what is more, the criteria of analysis and judgment are equally at stake in these battles).

This philosophical investigation into the structuring of historical time is inseparable from a concrete examination, which draws on a number of disciplines, of the modi operandi of the three key concepts indicated above. In each case, it is a matter of resituating these notions in the framework of the social, economic, and political practices that have shaped them. Lodging a challenge to Jean-François Lyotard's famous diagnosis in *The Postmodern Condition* (1979), according to which our epoch is the age of the end of grand narratives, this book aims at demonstrating that one of the most powerful historical imaginaries of our conjuncture still houses massive schemas of temporal organization purporting to grasp the meaning and direction of the story of time (*le sens de l'histoire*). It is not simply a matter of showing that the grand narratives of the past are still going strong, but rather of inquiring into their reconfiguration in the contemporary conjuncture. I am particularly interested in the curious destiny of the historical logic of Marxism, which was—if we are to believe Perry Anderson—the principal grand narrative criticized by Lyotard. For we are witnessing today, at least within certain sectors, an insidious recuperation of vulgar Marxist historiography (not to be confused with what Marx himself wrote) by a certain discourse of contemporary liberalism.

The first chapter of this book is dedicated to this central problematic, which it proposes to dissect by concentrating on a concept whose hour of glory corresponds to the moment in time at which neoliberalism rose to power (and to the perceived—but altogether relative—decline of Marxist discourses and practices): globalization. Invented, in principle, in order to take into account a series of phenomena generally judged to be new, if not inevitable and all-powerful, this concept allowed for a prodigious rehabilitation of three vulgar Marxist commitments. Summarizing in broad strokes, without the nuances that will be required below, we could say that this recuperation has replaced communism by "popular capitalism" (Margaret Thatcher) while preserving the essentials of Marxian historiography: (i) technico-economic determinism forcefully returns in the form of a Market—and the march of technologies—that imposes its laws in such a manner that we are obliged to follow them, whether we like it or not; (ii) the teleological conception of history is reinvented, and the totality of the past is henceforth organized around a linear trajectory of technico-economic progress leading to a sole and unique end: the so-called democratic freedom of free trade; (iii) the inevitable structure of history reappears in the inescapable and allegedly natural growth of modern technologies and of the neoliberal politico-economic order. This leads to the conclusion that a specter is haunting globalization, the specter of the very same Marxism that has supposedly been so often refuted by history, and more precisely by the history of so-called popular capitalism. The purported death of Marxism with the fall of the Berlin Wall and the rise of globalized neoliberalism has actually led to its phantom persistence in the very historical framework undergirding the reigning understanding of the present. Paraphrasing Marx's own famous paraphrase, in a repetition inciting us to pay more attention to the cunning repetitions of history, we might say that the contradictory mantra of globalization is "Marxism is dead, long live Marxism!" This paradox is not, however, a simple logical contradiction to be pointed out or celebrated as the aporia fragmenting our contemporary situation. It has formidable concrete effects insofar as it encourages the passivity of citizens before the inescapable forces of the presumed natural course of history while casting a shadow over those responsible for our supposed common destiny, thereby carefully preserving the status quo. It is therefore necessary to remind ourselves that globalization is not an undeniable and inevitable fact, nor is it a simple, deceptive illusion. It is an *idée-force*—a central forceful idea—anchored in a set of concrete practices that participate, to a greater or lesser extent, in the construction of a world-image. This chapter draws to a close, then, by sketching out a critique of this world-image that consists in demonstrating, among other things, that "the world" varies considerably according to space and social strata, which is particularly well illustrated by the ravages and discontents—to use Joseph Stiglitz's expression—of so-called globalization. It also insists on all of the rifts that have weakened, for quite some time already, this world-image, not to mention all of the forms of resistance and revolution that abound a bit all over "the world." It is of the utmost importance, in this regard, that what is called globalization has been accompanied by vast and diverse alter-globalization struggles.[7]

Since the first chapter initiates a critical reflection on the alleged technico-economic and political development of our conjuncture, it already sums up in many respects the basic problematic of the book as a whole. The subsequent chapters prolong this analysis by deepening the inquiry into technology and democracy. The second chapter concentrates more specifically on three conceptual oppositions that tend to coordinate a significant portion of the contemporary debate on the technological changes that apparently characterize our age: historical discontinuity and temporal continuity, autonomy and heteronomy, technophilia and technophobia. In each case, it proposes to break with these theoretical coordinates in order to outline a different approach to the question of contemporary technologies. Instead of searching, for instance, for the umpteenth epochal concept, or entering into the wearisome controversy over the continuity or discontinuity of this or that social phenomenon, it relies on an alternative historical order to think differently about the current status of technologies, notably by taking into account the three dimensions of history: the vertical dimension of time, the horizontal dimension of space and the stratigraphic dimension of the social practices of each space-time. This chapter insists, at the same time, on the fact that technology is not an isolated or isolatable phenomenon, and that it is therefore neither autonomous nor heteronomous. It is always intertwined with diverse sociohistorical practices. It could even be said that there is no technology in itself. There are only embedded technologies, which are linked in various ways to diverse practices and material institutions. In any case, we must acknowledge that it is not possible to judge technology as a whole from a technophile or technophobe point of view. It is necessary instead—this is the final argument of the chapter—to develop circumstantial judgments that are attentive to the ways in which "technologies" are intertwined in complex force fields and to the fact that social phenomena do not have absolutely univocal meanings. All in all, the critique of the conceptual coordinates of a large part of the debate on technology aims at opening channels for a new way of thinking technologies in our historical conjuncture.

The third chapter—which is by far the longest because it revisits and reframes various themes that traverse the book as a whole—raises a series of questions regarding the massive valorization of democracy in the dominant political imaginary, insofar as it is so categorical and absolute that it risks preventing any deep examination. A normative consensus imposes itself with such force in our conjuncture that it is extremely difficult to speak of democracy without assuming its intrinsic value, or even admitting that it is effectively the only legitimate form of government, if not the "end of history."[8] There is no need to accept Francis Fukuyama's demagogical thesis in order to be caught within the same political imaginary, as has been amply illustrated by the numerous critics of Fukuyama that have been content to play one form of democracy against another. In resisting this ideological pressure, this chapter thus proposes an untimely investigation that focuses on the ways in which democracy has become a value-concept whose normative force tends to subjugate its descriptive potential (to such an extent that the American government, for instance, can speak of its "democratic friends" while referring to some of the most repressive political regimes). In order to do this, it demonstrates that a veritable counter-history must be founded on a radical historicism, that is, the position according to which everything is historical, even if it is not reducible to strict historical determinants (as reductive historicism would have it). This allows us to distance ourselves from the prevailing political imaginary by resituating the obsession with democracy in the long history of political cultures. This chapter thereby sheds light on the historical contingency of the valorization of the concept of democracy, which is only approximately 150 years old (with important variations across space and social strata). It also insists on demonstrating the transformative power inherent in radical historicism insofar as it establishes the basis for a historical critique by denaturalizing the normative structures, affective networks, and intellectual givens of the contemporary conjuncture. It thereby resituates democratophilia in a triumphalist logic of history—in which we once again come across the notions of globalization and contemporary technology—that has imposed itself with formidable force over the last thirty years or so. Finally, it proposes to prolong the preceding analyses by elucidating the veritably political role played by the various attempts to purify the political, notably by isolating it from its inscription in specific socioeconomic and cultural worlds. Instead of beginning with the question of the best form of government *in general*, a question that almost inevitably leads today to the transfiguration of actually existing democracy into an absolute good independent of context, this chapter concludes by asking whether it would not be better to inquire into the elaboration of political practices in the broad sense of the term, meaning the collective constitutions of common worlds of values, norms, representations, institutions, and practices.

In summary, this book does not simply correct an image of the present judged to be false, by disclosing once and for all the truth of our era. Instead, it breaks with the historical order subtending a certain understanding of the contemporary world and proposes an alternative approach to the question of the specificity of our conjuncture. This counter-history of the contemporary thus not only invites the reader to call into question a conventional image of the present-day world as being characterized by the definitive triumph of globalization, technology, and democracy. It draws on an important body of literature and highly significant alternative praxes in order to incite a profound interrogation into the theoretical structures and the sociopolitical and economic practices that both produce and favor such a world-image. This is in order to be able to develop other historical orders and political imaginaries, and in this way to regain control—as some have already done to a very great extent—over the construction of our common histories and narratives (*nos histoires communes*), and more precisely over the forging of historical meanings and directions (*de sens historiques*) other than those imposed upon us.

CHAPTER 1

# A Specter Is Haunting Globalization

The concept of globalization imposes itself with such force today that its historical provenance has been concealed. The word seems to describe an undeniable reality by encapsulating—via a reckless desire for conceptual abbreviation—all of the new phenomena of our age, whether economic, political, social, cultural, industrial, or technological. Although the attempts to discern the onset and the precise characteristics of globalization are numerous, the debates around these nonetheless tend to obscure the provenance of the idea itself as well as of its conceptual and historiographical categories, as if forgetting the past was the key to understanding the present. Yet this past continues to weigh "like a nightmare on the brain of the living," and bringing it to light via counter-historical investigation will help provide new perspective on this apparently natural and necessary world-image.[1]

Globalization: Between Words and Things

We are repeatedly told that globalization has created a more unified world with a single economic market, a network of new technologies, the proliferation of a more or less homogeneous culture and novel structures of governance. Such a process is not only new, or at least relatively new; it is also supposedly inevitable—despite setbacks or slowdowns—given the nature of its driving forces and the general course of history. Looming over our existence like the dominant trait of a profound and widespread

*Zeitgeist*, globalization allows us to resist its consequences only if we are already subject to its effects. *Novel, inevitable, almighty*: such is the force that has supposedly been transforming our world from top to bottom.

Yet there is no agreement on the precise definition or the exact date of so-called globalization. To take only a few examples, can we really talk about a global information and communication system when regular Internet access is restricted, as I indicated in the introduction, to less than half of the planetary population (43.4 percent)?[2] Does a rhizomatic system of air transportation—mostly connecting major economic centers, airport hubs, and tourist sites—constitute a truly global system of transportation, especially considering all of the necessary documents (passports, visas, etc.) and the substantial financial resources required to use it? Are the archipelago of economic exchange[3] and the extremely unequal development of the planet signs of the existence of a global village?[4] Are the rejection of the treaty establishing a constitution for Europe and the presence of strong nationalist movements in European countries so many symptoms of a global age?[5] And what about the drastic increase in the number of slums since the end of the 1970s, which accounted for approximately a sixth of the population of planet Earth at the beginning of the twenty-first century (more than a billion people lived in slums in 2003 according to the report *The Challenge of the Slums*, published by the United Nations)? These shantytowns constitute, moreover, regions that are not only outside the preferred trajectories of the globe-trotters, but that are also sometimes disconnected from national and transnational governance, if not veritably "cut off from the world" (this is to say that there are several spaces in "the world" and that one of the fundamental problems haunting the notion of globalization is precisely that of reducing them to a single, more or less homogeneous spatiality).[6] Finally, how can we speak of the unification of planet Earth when so-called international organizations such as the World Bank and the International Monetary Fund have been responsible for redistributing wealth from the poorest countries to the richest ones?[7] Eric Hobsbawm reminds us, indeed, that "after twenty years of failing to pay attention to the social and human consequences of unfettered global capitalism, the president of the World Bank has come to the conclusion that for most of the world's population the word 'globalization' suggests 'fear and insecurity' rather than 'opportunity and inclusion.'"[8]

The defenders of globalization would probably argue that these issues are only temporary slowdowns in an inevitable process. Such a stance, rooted in a veritable historical faith, and often founded on a theodicy capable of integrating all of history's evils into a grand eschatological narrative, could, at least in principle, withstand the presentation of any series of empirical facts. It is therefore necessary to start by reminding ourselves that the notion of globalization is purely relative. Everything depends on the scale of analysis, the reference points, and ultimately on the question "Globalization *in relation to what*?" For some, the "discovery" of the "New World" at the end of the fifteenth century would be a sign of globalization, while for others globalization only began with the invention of mass communication and the spread of so-called post-Fordist capitalism. And in a few decades it is highly probable that such characteristics will be replaced by others (in situating ourselves in time, we should be wary of according an absolute privilege to the past, since the future constitutes a fundamental dimension of any history). There are no objective criteria that enable us to distinguish with precision true cases of globalization. In the absence of objective criteria of analysis, the participants in the globalization debate invent criteria in order to demonstrate the pertinence of their own distinctions between the global age and the preglobal era.

Let us take, as examples, two quotes:

Today, as commerce [and] travel [ . . . ] bring together diverse people, and their lifestyles are constantly being brought closer together through frequent communication, we see that certain national differences have diminished.

When has the whole earth ever so universally converged together *on so few united threads* as now? When have more *power* and *machinery* been possessed for shaking whole nations to the core with one *press*, with one *movement of a finger*?

Are these so many signs of globalization? Are not the overcoming of the national framework and the unification of the planet by commerce, travel, technology, and communication characteristics of globalization? Yet the authors do not explicitly refer to the process of globalization, and with good cause: the word did not yet exist. Despite what one might think (and in spite of the slightly dated language), these quotes were not randomly picked out from recent newspapers, nor do they appear in one of the numerous books devoted to the question of superseding the nation-state. They date from 1754 and 1774 respectively. Their authors are Jean-Jacques Rousseau and J. G. Herder.[9]

Does this mean that the reality of globalization precedes the invention of the term? This question touches on a fundamental philosophical problem that must be dealt with head-on: the relationship between words and things. There are two ideal-typical positions that are readily identifiable. The first, the realist position, is surely the dominant one in this domain. It consists in affirming that there is an autonomous world and that language is a system of communication enabling us to speak about it, if it be correctly or incorrectly. In this case, globalization would indeed be a real historical phenomenon and the late emergence of the term would simply correspond to an intellectual advance allowing us to talk more precisely and concisely about this reality. The second position, which might be qualified as lingua-centric, denies the existence of an autonomous reality and asserts that language is what delivers "the world" to us. Far from being a real phenomenon, globalization would simply be a term in a system of signification, a differential marker in a network of intralinguistic references.

It is advisable to distance ourselves from these two ideal-typical positions, founded on the opposition between language and reality, and ultimately on the dichotomy between human beings and the world (language often being conceived of as a human phenomenon). If an autonomous world existed independently from our practical, conceptual, perceptive, and discursive schemas (which seems more than probable), we would only have access to it through these. This does not come down to saying that the world is reducible to our apprehension of it or that we are free to construct reality from scratch. It means, rather, that the world only delivers itself to us as a world insofar as we are beings of the given world, with theoretico-practical dispositions and specific modes of experience. To cite one of Thomas Kuhn's distinctions to which I will return later, I would say that we never have a direct experience of stimuli or raw definitive facts. The primary elements of our experience are data, which present themselves as the lived, unquestioned givens of *our world*. As far as language is concerned, we should not consider it to be a largely autonomous and all-encompassing system that structures the totality of our thoughts and experience. Language is a dynamic and historical practice that, far from being an autonomous element, is intertwined with social, political, economic, and other practices. Hence the choice is not between *globalization as a word* and *globalization as a thing*. Nor should one accept as such the question that structures a significant portion of the globalization debate: is a word such as *globalization* appropriate for describing a thing such as the current state of the world?[10] What needs to be pointed out is that the notion of globalization emerges from practices linked to a specific schematization of the world, practices that have, moreover, been effective insofar as they have helped produce "the thing" supposedly described by "the word."

Marx's Unexpected Recuperation

By making the debate on globalization into a controversy regarding the relationship between a word and a thing, we promptly forget the historicity of the discursive, theoretical, and practical categories allowing us to apprehend "the historical real." In this respect, it is essential to recall that the emergence of the notion of globalization is very recent. Its origins date back to the 1950s and 1960s,[11] but it was in the 1980s and especially the 1990s that it started to impose itself as one of the key concepts of our conjuncture.[12] The number of articles in the *New York Times* discussing globalization can serve as an interesting barometer. Prior to 1970 there were no articles, and the statistics for the ensuing decades are relatively revealing: 1 article in the 1970s, 172 articles in the 1980s, 911 articles in the 1990s, and 3,012 articles between 2000 and 2010.[13] The results for other databases, such as *LexisNexis* or the archives of the *Washington Post* or the *Los Angeles Times*, follow the same pattern. We could also cite the number of works indexed under the keyword *globalization* in the Library of Congress, which confirm a similar, though deferred, tendency in the world of books: 1 book in the 1970s, 14 in the 1980s, 1,076 in the 1990s, and more than 10,000 between 2000 and 2010.[14] "'Globalization [*mondialisation*],'" writes Frédéric Lebaron, "has become in a few years one of the key notions of the economic and social debate. It is in particular at the beginning of the 1990s that the use of it spreads significantly in France, in competition with the word 'globalization [*globalisation*],' directly transposed from English."[15]

Instead of simply being a neutral concept used—or not—to describe new realities (other terms such as *internationalization* or *international development* were already available), it is a practical concept rooted in a very specific historical and geopolitical conjuncture, marked in particular by Ronald Reagan and Margaret Thatcher's politico-economic project, as well as by other important political and economic actors such as Paul Volcker (former chairman of the U.S. Federal Reserve), Augusto Pinochet, and Deng Xiaoping. This project was perfectly summed up by Thatcher's slogan: *There Is No Alternative*, or TINA.[16] This means at least two things at once: there is no *structural* alternative to the neoliberal economic system, and there is no *historical* alternative insofar as it is inscribed in the very destiny of this system to impose itself throughout the world. This obviously does not mean that every use of the concept of globalization is necessarily linked to the various metamorphoses of neoliberalism, but it is of the utmost importance to highlight the fact that the filiation of this concept is directly tied to the reconfiguration of the geopolitical world since the 1970s. This reconfiguration was fueled in the preceding decades by decolonization and later by the collapse of the Soviet Union. These two political events sometimes gave the impression that a world divided between imperial zones or ideological blocs[17] was giving way to a more and more unified planet, in which the reign of the alleged freedom of the free market promised, via an implacable theodicy, one market under God, indivisible, with liberty and justice (for some).[18] In other words, the concept of globalization is not a purely descriptive notion used to depict new historical phenomena. It is a concept linked— directly or indirectly—to a recent political imaginary and a new world-image in which the expansion of the free market is supposed to go hand in hand with the spread of freedom in the "crusade of popular capitalism."

This expression is borrowed from the speech that Margaret Thatcher presented at the Conservative Party Conference in 1986, which is in perfect alignment with the discourse in one of neoliberalism's manifestoes, Milton Friedman's *Capitalism and Freedom*: "The kind of economic organization that provides economic freedom directly, namely, competitive capitalism, also promotes political freedom because it separates economic power from political power and in this way enables the one to offset the other."[19]

In referring to globalization in what follows, I will therefore be focusing on the term's historical center of gravity, without pretending to sum up the totality of its uses. And by historical center of gravity I mean the linguistic practico-inert of the term, that is, the residues of former linguistic practices that, in becoming inert, continue to haunt the word and intervene in practices.[20] In short, the practico-inert of a term is a set of effects that produces effects.

The best explanation of the part played by this practical concept (at least at the level of its historical center of gravity) in the construction of a new world-image consists in underscoring the way in which this *praxi-concept* has surreptitiously and paradoxically appropriated a set of conceptual categories considered to be obsolete: those of vulgar Marxism. What I mean by this is a certain social idea of Marxism, which does not necessarily correspond to what Marx himself wrote.[21] Let us begin by outlining these categories, and we will later explore specific examples. According to a very widespread form of conventional wisdom, Marxism was refuted by history for at least three reasons:

(i) It was founded on a reductive technico-economic determinism.
(ii) It put forth a teleological conception of history in which the totality of the past was directed toward a single end, following a linear or dialectical trajectory of progress.
(iii) It held this teleological progress to be inevitable, like an organic process that historical actors would be incapable of stopping.

The "factual" refutation can also be summed up in three points:

(i) Technico-economic determinism failed because all capitalist societies did not engender communist revolutions.
(ii) History did not keep its promise insofar as its *telos*—the communist revolution as the harbinger of a classless society—actually produced totalitarian regimes that later collapsed, for the most part at the feet of democratico-capitalist countries.
(iii) The supposedly natural and inevitable evolution of history encountered significant resistance, including most notably from capitalism itself and from liberal democracies.

A veritable *Aufhebung* if ever there was one, the rehabilitation of this historical logic did not take place after the fact; it was already inherent in the apparent refutation of the Marxist vulgate. It is thus not only that the failure of yesterday becomes the success of today, but that the proof of the failure of the past already constitutes *in itself* the success of its burlesque recuperation. Let us summarize, a bit schematically, the devilish trick that "history" is trying to play on us, by resuscitating the tragedy of communism in the form of a farce, which is the farce of purportedly popular capitalism:

(i) Reductive technico-economic determinism reappears in the form of an all-powerful Market—allied with the unwavering march of technologies—that imposes its inescapable laws in such a way that we have to follow them whether we like it or not.[22]
(ii) Teleology returns in force, and the totality of the past is henceforth organized in a linear trajectory of technico-economic progress, leading to the sole and unique end of the freedom of free trade.
(iii) The inevitable structure of history resurfaces as the unavoidable and supposedly natural growth of modern technology and of the politico-economic system of neoliberalism.

Exactly as in vulgar Marxism, we find ourselves in a reductionist, teleological, and supposedly inevitable history: there is no alternative. Whatever we might try to do, the totality of history is apparently determined by an absolute law—the law of the market and of the march of technologies—implacably leading to a *telos*. A specter is haunting globalization, the specter of the very same Marxism that was supposedly refuted again and again by history, and more precisely by the history of capitalism.[23]

Here we find ourselves before a rebranding campaign on an unprecedented scale. The same basic product, deemed utterly obsolete and outdated, is recycled (as if by magic) under a new name and in a shiny package that render it almost unrecognizable. It is accompanied, as is appropriate, by a vigorous advertising campaign aiming, among other things, at concealing the product—which is to say, *that which has been produced*—behind the façades of marketing. Commodity-globalization fetishism, one might say, serves to mask the specter of Marxism. That this is a case of an economy of ideas changes very little, since the same elements and strategies are at work. At base, it would even be legitimate to speak of a repurposing campaign, which consists in taking the same fundamental historical and historiographical structures in order to use them for other ends, redirecting them to other objectives, and even to opposite goals.

We thereby jump, in a complete non sequitur, from one subject to the next, from communism to capitalism, without the slightest incident, or at least that is what this powerful advertising campaign would like us to believe.

Yet this is not all, because the historical order of our conjuncture is supposed to be even more profound, more real, more determinant, than that of the old-school Marxists. It is thus a matter of an inevitable and teleological determinism that is more fundamental and totalizing. It would thus apparently be capable of refuting Marxism itself, through a properly dialectical negation that purports to recuperate it at a higher, synthetic level. However, if Marxian historical logic was effectively refuted by history, and in particular by the history of globalization, and if the discourse of globalization has recuperated it in turn, this means in principle that the historical order of this discourse has always already been disproven. The tragic refutation of Marxism corresponds to the burlesque refutation—a refutation avant la lettre—of the farce that is the historical logic of the discourse of globalization.

In an oft-cited passage by Karl Marx, the latter declared, "Hegel remarks somewhere that all facts and personages of great importance in world history occur, as it were, twice. He forgot to add: the first time as tragedy, the second as farce."[24] He certainly did not expect that the history of Marxism would itself suffer the same fate. Yet nearly one century after the Russian Revolution, we have to admit that the ruse of history has done unprecedented work. For if the collapse of Soviet communism was largely perceived as a tragedy in relation to the hopes expressed at the beginning of the century, the recent history of so-called globalization ironically repeats the triumphalist historiography of vulgar Marxism. However, given the "failure" of the historical logic that it clandestinely recuperates, this "new" logic of history presents itself, in effect, as a veritable farce. According to its own proper criteria, it is necessary to draw the conclusion that it is more than destined for failure, precisely because it has *already* failed. The presumed tragedy of Marxism has been transformed, by an extraordinary phantasmatic renaissance more than 150 years after the prognostics of *The Eighteenth Brumaire of Louis Bonaparte*, into the farce of Fukuyama.

However, whereas a tragedy always implies a dénouement, and hence a veritable end, a farce can play itself out in perpetuity. In fact, it begins very precisely by playing and replaying, again and again—but as comedy—the tragedy of Marxism. Perhaps the most comic aspect of this burlesque repetition is that the alleged victory of "democratic" capitalism against Marxism has ultimately vindicated the latter. Indeed, it is as if what is often perceived as the triumph of globalization were only the coronation of Marxist historical logic (or, rather, of a certain Marxian logic of history). If the content has changed, it was to better preserve the form. We might even be tempted to draw the conclusion that it was precisely Marxism, in its crudest form, that won the Cold War: by withdrawing from the grandiose political stage of the confrontation between ideological blocs, it discreetly lodged itself in the minds of the victors, weighing "like a nightmare on the brain of the living," and particularly on the very same minds that strived to destroy it, to suppress it, or to repress it.[25] Are the defenders of globalization ultimately the best guardians of Marxism, and especially of the Marxian spirit, in the so-called post-Marxist age? Does this dialectical inversion of victor history require us to completely rethink the status of historical victors, particularly in the spectral times of the neoliberal farce?

This paradox of the real phantasmatic persistence of Marxism is not just a simple conceptual contradiction. It is also not an aporia to be soberly celebrated as the profound but inevitable framework fracturing our contemporaneity. On the contrary, it is part of a historical imaginary that functions as a powerful social system of understanding that situates us in time and in a space of possibility. It thus has formidable concrete effects, for it imposes with the force of law a certain vision of the world:

(i) It exonerates political and economic actors from any responsibility by insisting on the uncontrollable, inevitable, supposedly natural and desperately complex forces of the market and of the march of development.[26] History is thereby presented as a simple fatality. And who could be held responsible for what is inevitable, or even natural?

(ii) It promotes the passivity of citizens before their supposed common destiny by creating a climate of defeatist resignation. By hearing again and again that it is impossible to change our destiny, who would not end up believing it? Richard Sanders aptly writes regarding the repetitive mantra that globalization is inevitable: "This clever use of language serves two political purposes. First, if decision makers believe this mantra, they will develop policies that accord with what they see as 'inevitable' and turn this 'inevitability' into a self-fulfilling prophecy. Secondly, it creates a mood of resigned acceptance on the part of the population being impacted on by the structural changes flowing from economic liberalization."[27]

(iii) It carefully preserves the status quo by means of a conservative blackmail according to which any attempt to seriously change the course of history would be thoroughly senseless and would lead sooner or later to inadmissible crimes. Cornelius Castoriadis has perfectly summarized this blackmail: "Today, what dominates is resignation, even among the representatives of liberalism. What's the major argument at the moment? 'Perhaps this is bad, but the alternative is worse.' Everything boils down to this. And it's true that this has numbed quite a lot of people. They tell themselves: 'if we change things too much, we're headed for a new Gulag.' That's what's behind the ideological exhaustion of our age."[28]

The dominant historical imaginary is thus intimately linked to the reigning political imaginary. It imposes on us a world where we must content ourselves with being subjected to the effects of an implacable destiny without being able to identify those responsible nor hope to change its orientation. In the new global farce, history disguises itself as a veritable fatality.

The concept of globalization, at least in its historical center of gravity, reclaims supposedly defunct Marxist categories, in a historical conjuncture marked by the collapse of Soviet communism, in order to help create a new world-image in which the inevitable spread of the politico-economic project of neoliberalism is linked to abolishing the accountability of the historical actors at work behind this deployment and to the infantilization of those subjected to it. From this counter-historical point of view on globalization, it is imperative to reject the realist position as well as the lingua-centric position. Far from being a word that is purely descriptive of the real or a signifier in an autonomous system of signification, the term *globalization* is a forceful key idea (*idée-force*) of the last thirty or forty years that—intertwined with political, social, technological, and economic practices—has played a fundamental role in the imposition of a new world-image in which a determinist teleology dictates our destiny: we must follow the laws of the market! There is no alternative . . .

And yet our conjuncture has been marked by such an intense economic crisis that it was necessary—according to some of the most ferocious defenders of the so-called free-market economy—for the state to intervene in order to save the banking system, if not the entire economy. Martin Wolf, the author of *Why Globalization Works* (2004) and a highly regarded columnist for the *Financial Times*, announced, without beating around the bush, the reappearance of another phantom from the past: "The ghost of John Maynard Keynes [ . . . ] has returned to haunt us."[29] In attacking the reduction of the economy to a moral narrative, whether it be Austrian (Ludwig von Mises and Friedrich Hayek) or socialist, he categorically asserted: "We are all Keynesians now."[30] The journal *Esprit* spoke of "an ideological crash" of neoliberalism: "We are all in favor of regulation now! Since September 15, the date when the bankruptcy of the American bank Lehman Brothers was announced, it is impossible to keep track of the number of positions, across all of the ideological camps, in favor of the intervention of the state in the economy."[31] Naomi Klein, to cite a final example, drew an analogy between the financial crisis and the fall of the Berlin Wall by declaring that if the latter was the death knell of communism, then the former should be heard as the death knell of neoliberalism.[32]

However, it is important not to lose sight of exactly how the neoliberal system works. As David Harvey has demonstrated, by drawing on Karl Polanyi's masterful work, the free market has never been incompatible with state intervention, and the management of crises is part of the neoliberal project. We therefore need to inquire into how this crisis was presented by recalling, if we take the American example, that President George W. Bush kept forcefully repeating that the foundations of the economy were solid. Then suddenly, in the fateful month of September, as if faced with the sudden surge of a more or less unexpected "economic hurricane," he asked for $700 billion to avoid a severe economic meltdown. It was necessary to save the banks and businesses that were too big to fail. This complex crisis called for a reaction that was as fast as it was extreme, starting with $350 billion distributed by Treasury Secretary Henry Paulson, the former chairman and chief executive officer of Goldman Sachs.[33] We should note in passing that this sort of crisis discourse recalls all of the exceptional measures put in place or intensified after September 11, 2001: the USA PATRIOT Act, the Military Commissions Act, illegal wiretappings, extraordinary rendition, the network of secret prisons, the redefinition of torture by the Office of Legal Council, and so on.[34] It is not by chance that this crisis was presented as a complex and uncontrollable natural phenomenon, whose severity was largely unforeseen, for it is similar to the historical logic outlined above. By naturalizing the economy and transforming it into an autonomous authority independent of the decisions made by specific agents, this historical order promotes passivity (we can only bow before forces stronger than us), the removal of responsibility (no one can be held accountable for natural phenomena), and historical nearsightedness (the situation is so critical that we must respond quickly, without wasting time by debating over distant causes: time is short!).[35] If we were to step back and assess the overall situation, we would see numerous specters rising up in the cemetery that is neoliberalism, and we would need to begin questioning—following Polanyi—whether the very project of laissez-faire economics has ever been anything other than socialism for the rich or, more precisely, top-down class warfare enforced by state intervention.

Ideology and Political Imaginaries

The specter of vulgar Marxism has not only been haunting the concept and the discourse of globalization. It has also been at work behind the scenes of the theoretical debate, like the silent director of controversies. The "great globalization debate"—according to a well-known text by David Held and Anthony McGrew—is structured by an opposition between the "globalists" and the "skeptics," that is between those who believe in the reality of globalization and those who call it into question.[36] A certain Marxian concept of ideology is at the heart of this opposition, as the choice imposed on the participants in this debate is founded on the dichotomy between reality and ideological illusion. In fact, this is only the framework of ideology within vulgar Marxism, and it corresponds more precisely to the representational conception of ideology, which could be distinguished from the functionalist conception as well as the materialist conception.[37] The globalists' position is one of pure and simple realism: the concept of globalization refers to a historical reality. The skeptics' position consists in attacking the notion of globalization as an ideology whose purpose is to conceal the true nature of reality today.[38]

In another text from the same period written with David Goldblatt and Jonathan Perraton, Held and McGrew put forth a tripartite distinction to encompass the main positions in the globalization debate. The skeptical position is present once again, but the globalist position is divided into two distinct conceptions, identified respectively with the "transformationalists" and the "hyperglobalizers." The latter believe that globalization is mainly an economic process that has led to a denationalization of the economy. Although they oppose the skeptics by affirming that globalization is a reality rather than an illusion, they tend to agree with them on three essential points: the economy is the determinant in the last instance, history is linear and teleological, and historical development follows a more or less necessary trajectory.[39] Such tendencies show the extent to which these two positions, at least in their ideal-typical forms, are perfectly inscribed in the historical order outlined above, and most of the examples that they cite attest to the rehabilitation of vulgar Marxism in the debate on globalization. The "transformationalists," whose manifesto is without a doubt Anthony Giddens's *The Consequences of Modernity* (1990), break with economic determinism in the name of multicausal determinism by extending their analysis to the political, industrial, informational, military, cultural, and ecological developments of globalization. Giddens himself insists on the existence of four institutional dimensions of modernity: capitalism, industrialism, surveillance, and military power.[40] He affirms, moreover, that "modernity is inherently globalizing" and presents four dimensions of globalization: the capitalist world economy, the nation-state system, the world military order, and the industrial development of the planet.[41] Finally, "transformationalists" like Giddens object to the teleological and inevitable structure of history by insisting on its contingencies and on the impossibility of knowing its end.

It is important to highlight two aspects of this tripartite division. First of all, ideology remains an essential dividing line between the globalists ("hyperglobalizers" and "transformationalists") and the skeptics. Second, the split proposed by Giddens and his allies is only partial. The act of calling into question monocausal determinism, teleology, and the inevitable structure of history is surely an important step forward. And Gidden's multidimensional approach is as rich as his dialectic point of view and his holistic method. Yet it is important to ask why the "transformationalists" cling to the unifying conceptual category of globalization (as well as to that of modernity, at least in Giddens's case). If there is no unified and linear historical process but a plurality of developments, each following its own rhythm, then why group them together under the single label of "globalization"?[42] Why insist on the multidimensionality of reality and opposing—if not contradictory—tendencies, if this multidimensionality is not heterogeneous enough to escape the grip of a single word and concept (which, as we've seen, is far from being neutral, but rather functions as one of the slogans of the era marked by the collapse of Soviet communism)?[43] This short circuit between a multiple object and a single term reveals the extent to which the "transformationalists" rely on realism, and it attests to their lack of critical distance from forceful key ideas (*idées-forces*) like globalization or, in the case of Giddens, modernity and postmodernity.[44] By resituating this position in relation to the other two, we see that they ultimately represent—despite the exceptions that exist in all three camps—variants of a realist thesis: globalization is primarily an economic reality ("hyperglobalizers"); it is a multidimensional reality ("transformationalists"); it is an illusion hiding the true reality of our times ("skeptics").

In relation to this tripartite division, the reader might have the impression that I am here staking out a position that could easily be inscribed in the skeptical framework by being summed up as follows: globalization does not in fact exist but is rather a powerful ideological construct that aims at hiding the deliberate expansion of neoliberalism. If that were the case, globalization would be an ideological illusion manipulated by malevolent powers trying to impose a false image of the world in order to advance a highly questionable project. Such a thesis would be based, moreover, on a conception of ideology characterized by three traits: (i) ideology would be an intentional phenomenon insofar as it would be rooted in malicious motives and strategies of manipulation; (ii) it would be an intellectual construct, for those using it as well as for those subjected to it and those who resist it; (iii) it would be inscribed in an epistemological opposition between the true and the false, as well as in an ontological dichotomy between reality and illusion. Intentional, intellectual, and structured by the opposition between truth and lies, the ideology of globalization would be a mask imposed on the world by the ill-intentioned.[45]

Such an understanding of globalization deserves to be considered in order to interpret and shed light on the flamboyant success of this fetishized notion. But it nonetheless risks missing what is most essential. To clearly underscore the differences between the skeptical position presented by Held and McGrew, and the position taken here, I would like to propose a distinction between ideology and political imaginary. Unlike an ideology, or rather the notion of ideology outlined above, a political imaginary is a practical mode of intelligibility of politics, that is, a world vision anchored in agents' practical sense. Although there can be intentional attempts at manipulation, a political imaginary is constituted at a more ingrained level than ideology insofar as it is made up of a set of practical dispositions acquired by participation in a social world.[46] Such dispositions are part of the common sense of social agents, and they are not limited to the conceptual domain. A political imaginary is also composed of discursive, perceptive, affective, normative, and practical dimensions. It is a way of being in the political world, and that is why it is incompatible with the opposition between reality and illusion. The real is not on one side with ideological illusions on the other. There are world-images interwoven with practical, discursive, and perceptive dispositions.[47] A world-image is not, strictly speaking, an image of the world, for at least two good reasons: there is not *one* given world behind all images, and each world-image is the construction of a veritable world unto itself. If this is a perspectivalism, it is not at all a perspectivalism situated in a global space shared by everyone. It is a formative perspectivalism in which each perspective—which is irreducible to individual vantage points—constitutes a world. To return to the question of political imaginaries, we must therefore recognize that there are a plurality of them, even if there are some that ardently strive—and to what an extent!—to crush others (and they are, moreover, irreducible to a single determinant, such as the economic mode of production). Political imaginaries are, moreover, constitutively flexible. Instead of imposing themselves from above or as a whole, like an ideology in the singular, they adapt themselves to and are adapted to specific situations. This is a case of ready-to-wear, or rather ready-to-think, and all imaginable sizes and colors are available.

I would not deny, for all that, that the concept of globalization can play an ideological role. On the contrary, it has certainly been mobilized for ideological ends. However—and this is the main point I wanted to emphasize—it is at the level of the political imaginary that the concept has truly taken root. Indeed, even those who ignore or openly reject neoliberal ideology, or those who recognize all of the damaging effects of "globalization," often inscribe themselves—in spite of their intentions and in diverse ways—within the political imaginary of globalization. In this sense, the distance taken from a certain ideology does not at all amount to a break with the political imaginary in which it is rooted. One of the aims of this counter-history is precisely to dismantle the political imaginary that imposes itself in our conjuncture in order to create space for the emergence of other imaginaries, if they are already formed, or if they remain to be constructed.

Hence, instead of taking a position in the globalization debate, we should rather take a position *on* this debate by breaking with the realism that underlies it and by resituating it in its historical conjuncture. To be more precise, let us recall the distinction that Thomas Kuhn proposes between stimuli and data. In a series of remarkable analyses, he shows that we never have direct experience of stimuli, and thus of reality in its pure form. The primary elements of our experience are constituted by data. This does not mean, however, that we are free to choose or invent the world we would like, but rather that the world delivered to us can only be *our* world, the world of our data, because "a given world, whether everyday or scientific, is not a world of stimuli."[48] Regarding globalization, I would say, for my part, that it is neither a unique or differentiated reality, nor a word simply constructing a false reality. As the history of the term demonstrates, as well as the ways in which it is intertwined with diverse sociopolitical and economic practices, the concept of globalization is a datum of the dominant political imaginary. It is a fundamental dimension of a new world-image, which has been imposing itself with formidable force over the past thirty years or so.

Putting an End to a Globalizing Concept?

Globalization functions, in the reigning political imaginary, as a globalizing concept meant to summarize all or nearly all of the economic, technological, political, social, and cultural phenomena of our times. Even the harshest critics of this commanding concept sometimes reproduce the political imaginary on which it depends. How, then, can we break with such a concept? Since it is not a matter of an ideology in the sense of a deceptive representation, we cannot be satisfied with a simple appeal to the reality behind illusions by opposing science to ideology. Rather, we must dismantle "the given world," that is, the common ecosystem produced by a world-image and inscribed in the practical common sense of the prevailing political imaginary of our historical conjuncture.

For the purposes of this chapter, I will limit myself to indicating three forms of critique—which have already been at work in diverse ways in what precedes—that can serve to support a break with "the given world."[49] Historical critique, to begin with, consists in stepping back from "our present" by resituating it in a historical perspective. Instead of using the past to justify our own image of the present, we should try rather to establish distance from ourselves by examining our present as if we were historians, or, better yet, ethnologists, from a distant age. As in some of Jean Rouch's films, we should undertake an ethnology of ourselves and an anthropology of the present by recognizing that our social practices are no less contingent than those of societies practicing animism or pantheism. Such a perspective requires a radical historicism, that is, a historicism that recognizes that everything is historical, including all of the things that seem to be most natural in our thoughts, feelings, discourses, and practices. This is precisely one of the objectives of this book. By retracing the history of the concept of globalization and its diverse links to the history of neoliberalism, as well as to the Marxist historical logic supposedly refuted by this history, I want to shed a different light on our contemporary situation and on the historical order of the dominant political imaginary.

The second form of critique is historiographical, and it directly attacks the historical order or logic haunting discourses on globalization. It is very interesting to note in this regard that we can find all of the necessary tools for a critique of economism, teleology, and historical inevitability in the Marxist, Marxian, and post-Marxist traditions. Friedrich Engels explicitly marked the distance between Marxism and economism, notably in his correspondence with Joseph Bloch in 1890. Moreover, Marx's letter on Russia speaks volumes on his own position—at least in this text since his corpus is not homogeneous—in relation to historical determinism and purportedly transhistorical laws. Responding directly to the author of the article "Karl Marx Before the Tribunal of Zhukovsky," he writes:

> What application to Russia could my critic draw from my historical outline? Only this: if Russia tries to become a capitalist nation, in imitation of the nations of western Europe, *and in recent years she has taken a great deal of pains in this respect*, she will not succeed without first having transformed a good part of her peasants into proletarians; and after that, once brought into the lap of the capitalist regime, she will be subject to its inexorable laws, like other profane nations. That is all. But this is too much for my critic. He absolutely must needs metamorphose my outline of the genesis of capitalism in western Europe into a historico-philosophical theory of the general course, fatally imposed upon all peoples, regardless of the historical circumstances in which they find themselves placed, in order to arrive finally at that economic formation which insures with the greatest amount of productive power of social labor the most complete development of man.[50]

Let us briefly consider, as well, two contemporary examples. In one of his best-known texts, "Marxism and Revolutionary Theory" (1964–65), Cornelius Castoriadis attacked the classical forms of Marxian philosophy of history by calling into question technico-economic determinism, as well as the inevitable structure of historical teleology.[51] Such an understanding of history purports to isolate the technological domain as an autonomous sphere with its own proper laws, whereas for Castoriadis "no technical fact has an assignable meaning if it is isolated from the society in which it is produced and none imposes a univocal and ineluctable meaning on the human activities it underlies."[52] He calls into question, at the core of his critique, the reduction of creation to a purely determined activity: "History cannot be thought according to the determinist schema (nor, moreover, according to a simple 'dialectical' schema), because it is the domain of *creation*."[53] Making room for creation, and hence unpredictability, does not however mean falling prey to absolute relativism or descending into the chaos of an utterly incomprehensible history. Castoriadis refers, for instance, to a non-spiritualist and non-materialist dialectic that "must set aside the rationalist illusion, seriously accept the idea that the infinite and the indefinite exist, and admit—without for all that giving up on the work to be done—that every rational determination leaves a non-determined and non-rational residue, that the residue is just as essential as what has been analyzed, that necessity and contingency are continually intertwined with one another."[54]

In *Hegemony and Socialist Strategy* (1985), Ernesto Laclau and Chantal Mouffe review the history of Marxism and its theoretico-practical consequences. While rightly insisting on the diversity of the Marxist tradition, they highlight several failures of classical Marxism. It could not demonstrate, for instance, that socialism was the necessary consequence of the collapse of capitalism. It is indeed impossible, in their opinion, to prove the existence of a link between socialism and the end of capitalism because history is not simply an objective process. They thereby reject Marxist historical determinism and insist on the role played by subjectivity in historical developments. Moreover, classical Marxism reduces political subjects to "class subjects," whereas "democratic" struggles are not necessarily limited to questions of class for them. In so doing, it tends to reduce politics to an economic base, despite the fact that the political is irreducible to the economic. In short, their deconstructivist critique consists in rejecting historical determinism, economism, and the reduction of political subjectivity to a class issue. The underlying problem is what they call *essentialist apriorism*—a problem that extends well beyond Marxism—which consists in believing that privileged points of reference (the end of history, the economy, the class subject) escape from social struggles.

Although these various forms of critique are intertwined and interrelated, we can nevertheless distinguish a third type: economic and political critique. To begin with, such a critique should evaluate globalization according to its own criteria. I will not here get into the concrete consequences of our allegedly common destiny, which have been well documented.[55] I will instead limit myself to referring to an incisive critique that has the advantage of putting economic and political analysis in historical perspective. I have in mind Karl Polanyi's masterful work *The Great Transformation*, in which he brilliantly attacks the historical credo of the advocates for liberal economics, that is, the idea that the laissez-faire economy was somehow a natural development, whereas the resistance to it was the result of deliberate and concerted action by the opponents of economic liberalism. Breaking with orthodoxy, Polanyi shows the extent to which the establishment and preservation of the free market necessitates, and has necessitated, state intervention: "As long as that system [the market system] is not established," he writes in a passage that should make us reflect on the recent financial crisis, "economic liberals must and will unhesitatingly call for the intervention of the state in order to establish it, and once established, in order to maintain it."[56] This is why, as he adds in a passage that deserves to be foregrounded in our day and age: "The accusation of interventionism on the part of liberal writers is [ . . . ] an empty slogan, implying the denunciation of one and the same set of actions according to whether they happen to approve of them or not. The only principle economic liberals can maintain without inconsistency is that of the self-regulating market, whether it involves them in interventions or not."[57] And on the relationship between the market economy and state intervention, he is absolutely clear: "The road to the free market was opened and kept open by an enormous increase in continuous, centrally organized and controlled interventionism."[58] Furthermore, he demonstrates how the rejection of economic liberalism, far from being an anti-liberal conspiracy rooted in collective monetary interests, cropped up as a spontaneous and generalized reaction arising from the threat posed by the autonomization of the economy in relation to the social fabric. This threat comes from the principal novelty introduced by the historical emergence of the so-called self-regulating market, in which human beings and nature became objects of commerce: "The control of the economic system by the market is of overwhelming consequence to the whole organization of society: it means no less than the running of society as an adjunct to the market. Instead of economy being embedded in social relations, social relations are embedded in the economic system."[59] Polanyi perfectly summarizes his attack on the orthodox vision of the history of the market economy by highlighting a dual paradox: "While *laissez-faire* economy was the product of deliberate state action, subsequent restrictions on *laissez-faire* started in a spontaneous way. *Laissez-faire* was planned; planning was not."[60]

These historical, historiographical, economic, and political critiques provide us with the necessary tools to break with the globalizing concept of globalization, and thus call into question the historical order structuring the reigning political imaginary. They thereby contribute to a counter-history of globalization, understood not only as a fundamental criticism of the world-image that it sustains and favors, but more profoundly as the systematic dismantling of the historical order on which it depends. For this order, by surreptitiously rehabilitating Marxian historiography (an inexorable ghost), establishes a formidable teleological determinism. It encourages the passivity of citizens in the face of the inescapable forces driving the supposedly natural course of history, while at the same time casting a shadow over those responsible for our "common destiny." It subjects us to an appalling—and dishonest—blackmail according to which any attempt to truly change the course of history would be responsible for *all of the consequences*, including the violent reactions of those who refuse change. It is therefore necessary to recall, to begin with, that history does not have a single meaning or direction, and that globalization is not an undeniable or inevitable fact, or even a deceptive illusion. It is a social signifier and a forceful key idea (*idée-force*) linked to a set of concrete practices that participate, directly or indirectly, in the construction and preservation of a world-image. Rooted in common sense, it is so powerful that it tends to dictate our future by means of an implicit theodicy. Yet, as we have seen, if we conclude from the alleged historical collapse of Marxism that there is no alternative to popular capitalism, the conclusion we draw perfectly inscribes itself in the same historical logic that was purportedly refuted by history (according to the defenders of popular capitalism). Ultimately, the only logical lesson to draw is that *history is not destiny*, since even the prophets, be they vulgar Marxists or globalists, are caught in the whirlwind of time.

CHAPTER 2

# Are We Really Living in a Technological Era?

This age is the era of technology. Born of the industrial revolution, it poses anew the question of technics, which is henceforth evident to everyone.
—Bernard Stiegler

It is generally accepted that we live in a new technological era. Regardless of whether this is qualified in terms of the computer revolution, the digital transformation, or new information and communication technologies (ICT), it is impossible to ignore the common discourse postulating that a historical evolution is purportedly disrupting our world. Most of the time, it is affirmed in no uncertain terms that we are dealing with an unprecedented situation, but some proclaim, going against this trend, that the specificity of our epoch is explained by the fact that it has roots in a long-standing tradition, whether it be that of modern capitalism or that of Western metaphysics.[1] In both cases, new concepts are invented to attempt to grasp the singularity of the present time, such as the postmodern condition, control societies, the precession of simulacra, or the world of speed. At times technology is identified as the veritable source of this new configuration; at other times it is seen to be, instead, a major symptom of deeper determinants. In any event, the conceptualization of the role of technology in the contemporary world almost always goes hand in hand with the adoption of a normative standpoint, whether it be an overt celebration, a virulent condemnation, a simple tone of denigration or praise, or even a "balanced" point of view seeking to take both sides into consideration.

This is the way the conceptual coordinates of an important part of the current debate on contemporary technology are laid out. Three conceptual oppositions organize a theoretical playing field that allows for a nearly infinite number of positions: historical discontinuity or temporal continuity, autonomy or heteronomy, technophilia or technophobia. Intermediate and hybrid positions should not deceive us regarding what is most essential, for the conceptual coordinates always leave an important margin of maneuver. They organize, more generally, an ecology of the mind by drawing up a map of the space of possibilities, which is obviously not unrelated, as we shall see, to social and political ecology.

Far from seeking to take a position in this debate on technology and the present, I propose here to reconsider the conceptual coordinates that organize it in order to break the relative consensus—which is, of course, by no means ubiquitous—and sketch out other ways of approaching the present and the question of technology.

## The Historical Logic of the Technological Era

The debate on technology most often relies on a vertical historical logic in which the horizontal dimension of space disappears behind the singular thread of time. If it be continuous or discontinuous, if the discontinuities be abundant or rare, all of this matters relatively little in relation to the fundamental issue at stake: history is conceived of only according to its chronological dimension, at the expense of the geographic diversity of historical developments. It is just such a logic that allows us to reduce the complexity of history to the model of time periods and to surrender ourselves to the epochal thinking so dear to the never-ending discussions on the nature of the present. Periodic historical logic assumes that time is structured by more or less homogeneous epochs—or by a single grand era—allowing us to determine the nature of a particular age and grasp it with a single concept. This is indeed the crux of epochal thought, which inevitably sinks into conceptual ambivalences and semantic vagaries by pretending to become the faithful representative of so many diverse phenomena. For a single concept can only summarize the totality of what is happening in the world at a given point at the price of becoming a container concept that is too vague and elastic to be relevant. In this regard, many theses about the so-called technological age resemble those of the incessant debates on the nature of the present. The starting point of such controversies is precisely a periodic historical order and an epochal thinking that claims to be able to use a single concept—such as postmodernism, globalization, the era of emptiness or insignificance—to summarize all or nearly all of the activities of a historical period. They thereby forget the horizontal dimension of history, namely the geographic diversity of practices at a given time (not to mention what I propose to call the stratigraphic dimension, since geographic locations are not homogeneous).[2] Consider in this regard the following statement by Bernard Stiegler: "This extraordinary acceleration of technical development, which has become technological, today produces, *in the totality of the world population*, a feeling of immense disorientation."[3] How can such a general and categorical declaration be verified? Is a single concept really capable of summing up a particular, non-trivial aspect of the totality of the world population?

In this regard, let us take a moment here to consider an article by Gilles Deleuze that is often cited in discussions of contemporary technologies: "Postscript on Control Societies" (1990). In this text, he sketches a picture of three great eras based on an interpretation of the work of Michel Foucault: the age of societies of sovereignty (before the eighteenth century), the era of disciplinary societies (from the eighteenth century to the early twentieth) and the epoch of control societies (from World War II). Such a periodic history forms the backdrop for a reflection on the specificity of our era, which Deleuze proposes to think by means of the epochal concept of control. This is supposed to be the unifying axis for an almost infinite number of phenomena that allegedly stand together as part of the same historical movement: the crisis of spaces of confinement (prison, hospital, factory, school, family), the emergence of new forms of control (high-speed, short-term, with rapid turnover, etc.), the powerful rise of companies, the strong presence of lifelong training and continuous assessment, the preponderance of unlimited procrastination, the predominance of numbers, the disappearance of the couple mass-individual in favor of "dividuals" and samples, the proliferation of computing machines, the domination of overproduction capitalism, a new medicine "without doctor or patient," and so on.[4] The concept of control society is so elastic and easy to manipulate that it can purport to connect so many heteroclite phenomena in a more or less coherent ensemble. In doing so, however, it loses its power of discrimination, since the link between all of these disparate elements sometimes seems to depend more on free association than on a rigorous demonstration. When Deleuze asserts, for instance, that "we've gone from one animal to the other, from the mole to the snake, in the system in which we live," one realizes the elasticity of the container concept of control: "The old monetary mole is the animal of spaces of confinement, but the snake is the animal of societies of control."[5] In losing its power of discrimination in a conceptual malleability without apparent limits, it simultaneously abolishes safeguards against the most debatable conclusions. Let us cite but two particularly striking examples: "Man is no longer confined man, but indebted man" and "The man of disciplines was a discontinuous producer of energy, but the man of control is rather wave-like, put in orbit, on a continuous beam. Everywhere surfing has already replaced the old sports."[6] Obviously, we should not lose sight of the dose of playful provocation in such pseudo-prophetic declarations and this homily on animals. Yet the idea that "man"—an altogether problematic unifying concept—is no longer being confined in our time is absurd. Prisons were not at all disappearing in 1990, as evidenced by the fact that the prison population in France doubled between 1975 and 1995, reaching around fifty-four thousand inmates according to a study conducted by Pierre Tournier.[7] And what are we to say about the current situation, where prison overcrowding is breaking its own records (with some sixty-three thousand inmates in France)?[8] Without discussing all of the recent revelations regarding Guantánamo, Abu Ghraib, and the secret CIA prisons, let us recall that the United States, which is the country with the highest per capita incarceration rate in the world, has a prison population of 2.2 million people (according to the 2014 Human Rights Watch *World Report*).[9] If "confined man" is very far from having disappeared, then what about the idea that surfing has already replaced old sports? What is the value of such provocative suggestions without an evidential basis? What link is there really between surfing and control society apart from the letter *s* (as in *s*nake)?

 I should clarify, particularly in relation to the discussion of ideology in the previous chapter, that I am here relying on a social epistemology rather than on an idea of purely objective truth. Far from being a transcendent form, truth is a site of social struggles. However, this does not mean in the least that "everything is relative," as some like to say in order to immediately prevent any reflection on the social stakes of veracity. There are truth practices that are recognized as legitimate in certain sectors, even if they remain fallible at the end of the day. Demonstration based on evidence is one of these, in this case, and if I am appealing to any objectivity, it is a concrete objectivity, meaning an objectivity upheld by certain social communities because of their practices of truth.

Moreover, it is not a matter here of knowing whether we are truly in control societies or if another epochal concept would be better suited to our era. It is rather an issue of rejecting the methodological basis for such questions. Taking into account the horizontal dimension of history breaks the logic of periods by showing in fact that there is a variable distribution of phenomena depending on historical space. To take a "technological" example: according to the International Telecommunication Union of the United Nations, 77.6 percent of the European population and 66 percent of the population in North and South America have regular Internet access, yet only 20.7 percent of the African population and 36.9 percent of the population in the Asia-Pacific region have such access.[10] In the least developed countries in the world, which include a population of 940 million people, only 9.5 percent use the Internet.[11] To speak of the computer age in regions where a minority of the population is directly affected seems somewhat excessive. And we should remind ourselves in this regard that only 43.4 percent of the world population has regular Internet access.[12] The basic problem is that historical activity remains irreducible to singular concepts. It is not only that the horizontal dimension of history is such that robust geographic diversity comes to call into question the idea of a simple march of time where epochs would succeed one another in an interlocking sequence. It is that the search for a single concept—computing, technology, technics, control, and so on—to capture the essence of an age remains illusory. Contrary to what the defenders of epochal thinking would like to believe and to have others believe, there is no periodic essence that could be grasped once and for all with a single idea. There is no *Zeitgeist* or spirit of the times, since, precisely, there is no spirit unifying all of the historical activities at a given moment. To really think the "present time," we must break with the historical essentialism and conceptual reductionism of epochal thought. It is necessary to try and chart a complex topography that cannot be placed under the umbrella of a single temporal category or a unique concept. We have to face—this is indeed one of the tasks of a counter-history—the temporal, spatial, and social splintering of historicity.

Yet someone will undoubtedly object—to return to the example of the Internet—that if it has not yet spread in Africa and Asia like in the Americas and Europe, it is only a question of time. For the inevitability of technological evolution appears to be an undeniable feature of our present. It would suffice to recall the astonishing changes between 2000 and 2015: Internet access increased from 400 million people to 3.2 billion.[13] In this regard, we should pause here a moment to comment on Jean-François Lyotard's work in order to underscore how wrong he was to declare in 1979 that our age was the era of incredulity regarding metanarratives. Without dwelling on the very tight argumentative structure of *The Postmodern Condition* (which I have had the opportunity to do elsewhere), it is clear that the discourse on the inevitable progress of technology—like globalization discourse—resembles, in many respects, what he called a metanarrative. It is indeed an eschatological discourse organized around an Idea to come, or even always still to come: technological perfection (or global unification). This discourse, like all metanarratives, purports to tell the truth about history by discerning the true course of events. Finally, it is founded on a meta-subject whose role is to unify the totality of history into a single and unique trajectory: technology itself as force of innovation (or the free market). All said and done, if one wanted to use Lyotard's vocabulary (which is not, however, without its problems), one could say that the story of technological progress—or of the spread of globalization—is one of the most powerful grand narratives of our historical conjuncture. It makes technology, in certain cases, into a panacea capable of overcoming the most serious of problems, if it be the destruction of the earth, global warming, old age, or unemployment. In the most extreme cases, technological theodicy even manages to justify the continuation of harmful practices hastening the devastation of the planet and our own ruin. For all of the evils of the world would never be able to call into question a truth more profound than any other: technology will save us like a veritable deus ex machina!

Several things should be remembered in this regard. First of all, as Cornelius Castoriadis has so clearly demonstrated, "technology does not necessarily progress in an uninterrupted fashion."[14] There may be advances or setbacks depending on the space-time. And the distribution of technologies—apart from a few notable exceptions—is quite closely linked to income distribution and to the uneven development of the planet.[15] Rather than speak of an inevitable evolution, we should thus take into account the actual distribution of phenomena according to the logic of historical metastases, that is, variable-rate transformations that are unevenly distributed in space and time. We can thereby highlight the diverse ways in which some strata of existence, for certain people, have effectively been modified, without falling into abstract generalities. This is a very important point that deserves emphasis. Indeed, I fully acknowledge that there have been significant changes in some aspects of the lives of a certain number of people, and this is one reason I am calling for a precise stratigraphic analysis rather than general diagnoses. Second, the distribution of technologies and the production of new technologies are so intertwined with economic and political stakes, as well as with the uses that are made of them, that it is utterly illusory to think that technological progress is the result of an autonomous and inevitable process (I will return to this later). "Technological innovation," as Samir Amin quite rightly asserts, "is certainly not socially neutral, since its application is governed by the logic of profitability."[16] Moreover, it is not because a technology exists that it will be used on a large scale, as is amply illustrated by the case of alternative technologies (solar panels, wind turbines, etc.). What is more, use can entirely transform technological mechanisms and is thus an integral part of their development, which calls into question—as Janet Abbate has powerfully demonstrated in the case of the Internet—the very distinction between production and consumption or use.[17] Third, technology is not all-powerful, despite what a certain mythology would have us believe. It is not only that it is unable to solve all problems, but also that in overcoming certain difficulties, it can produce others (the case of the pollution caused by the internal combustion engine is a glaring example). Fourth, history is not fatality since the course of time is not prescribed. Trends visible today could be reversed tomorrow. History is not at all natural insofar as it depends on a constant production and reproduction of what exists. It is for this reason, among others, that James Curran is absolutely right to point out, with numerous examples to support his claim, that "the impact of the internet does not follow a single direction dictated by its technology. Instead the influence of the internet is filtered through the structures and processes of society."[18] In this light, the conclusion of this excellent book, which he co-wrote with Natalie Fenton and Des Freedman, should also be cited: "Although it was said, and continues to be said, that the internet was going to virtually single-handedly change the world, this has not been the case. Like all previous technologies, its use, control, ownership, past development and future potential are context dependent."[19] Finally, the supposedly inevitable evolution of technology presupposes that the latter is an isolatable phenomenon, that there is something like technology in itself. It is to this idea that we should now turn in order to examine it in the light of the opposition between autonomy and heteronomy.

Technological Essentialism in Question:
Autonomy or Heteronomy

The idea of an inevitable historical evolution of technology is generally founded on a conceptualization of it as an isolatable fact. It may be the source of an apparently natural process or the symptom of more profound causes. In the first case, it is technology *itself* that is supposedly at the origin of so many transformations insofar as it is the determinant in the last instance or the motor of history. Such a thematization purports indeed to isolate the technical domain as an autonomous sphere with its own proper laws. In the second instance, technology maintains its internal coherence as an isolatable phenomenon but is shown to be determined by external forces. *Determined technology* opposes itself to *technological determinism*.

Let us take the example of the critique of Walter Benjamin formulated by Jacques Rancière in *The Politics of Aesthetics*. In the latter's opinion, Benjamin reversed the relation between art and technology by deducing artistic properties from technical attributes. The position that he takes is rooted, according to Rancière, in one of the common assumptions of modernism: the distinction between the arts is founded on technical and material differences. Against this thesis, the author of *The Politics of Aesthetics* asserts that the mechanical arts can only be recognized as such within a regime of identification in which the hierarchies between genres and subjects have been dismantled in favor of expressive equality.

The aesthetic regime of art, which came into being toward the end of the eighteenth century, dismantled the hierarchies of the system of representation by making room for the art of the commonplace, where anything whatsoever can become art. Rancière thus proposes to invert Benjamin's thesis by asserting that it is this new artistic regime that made possible the recognition of the mechanical arts qua *arts*. He thereby counterposes a thesis founded on determined technology to what he perceives as Benjamin's technological determinism. "On the one hand," Rancière writes, "the technological revolution comes after the aesthetic revolution. On the other hand, however, the aesthetic revolution is first of all the honor acquired by the commonplace, which is pictorial and literary before being photographic or cinematic."[20]

According to Raymond Williams's judicious analyses, one should reject technological determinism as well as determined technology. Truth be told, technology is neither a determinant in the last instance nor an element fully determined by external forces. This is the case for several reasons. In the first place, in order to understand what we call technology, we cannot separate it from social practices. The isolation of technology is in fact an abstraction, for no technology exists independently of its social, cultural, and historical inscription.[21] It is for this reason that it is perhaps useful to invoke the concept of social ecology, in the sense of the organization of a shared world that—in this particular case—produces, distributes, and makes use of diverse technologies. According to Murray Bookchin, who proposed the term *social ecology* to express "the conviction that nearly all our present ecological problems originate in deep-seated social problems": "Technologies consist not only of the devices humans employ to mediate their relationship with the natural world, but also the attitudes associated with these devices. The attitudes are distinctly social products, the results of the social relationships humans establish with each other."[22] In the second place, social determination remains irreducible to monocausal determinism. Despite the reassuring cohesion of such a schema, the complexity of social dynamics is such that it is impossible to identify a sole and unique cause behind a particular phenomenon. Third, not only is technology situated in a network of causes and effects, but these also vary considerably based on the situation. By consolidating technology as a unique element, abstracted from the social world, one risks effacing the dynamism of its existence and the variability of its effects. On this issue, it is worth citing *in extenso* Williams's thesis:

> Technological determinism is an untenable notion because it substitutes for real, social, political and economic intention, either the random autonomy of invention or an abstract human essence. But the notion of a determined technology has a similar one-sided, one-way version of human process. Determination is a real social process, but never (as in some theological and some Marxist versions) a wholly controlling, wholly predicting set of causes. On the contrary, the reality of determination is the setting of limits and the exertion of pressures, within which variable social practices are profoundly affected but never necessarily controlled. We have to think of determination not as a single force, or a single abstraction of forces, but as a process in which real determining factors—the distribution of power or of capital, social and physical inheritance, relations of scale and size between groups—set limits and exert pressures, but neither wholly control nor wholly predict the outcome of complex activity within or at these limits, and under or against these pressures.[23]

Faced with the conceptualization of technology as an isolatable element, it is necessary to remind ourselves, indeed, that technology does not exist *in itself*. What is called "technology" is a set of phenomena identified as similar according to a conceptual demarcation proper to a specific sociohistorical conjuncture. It is very tightly connected to a whole series of social, political, economic, and other practices. It is therefore necessary to reject technological essentialism in all of its forms: there is no technology in itself; there are only "technological" phenomena that are identified as such within diverse practices. As Castoriadis rightly reminds us, "No technical fact has an assignable meaning if it is isolated from the society in which it is produced, and none imposes a univocal and ineluctable sense and direction on the human activities that it underlies, even those closest to it."[24]

Let us take a specific example of the theoretical faux pas favored by the desocialization (and the dehistoricization) of "technology." In order to show that philosophy is dependent upon technology, Bernard Stiegler examines "the birth of philosophy," which he identifies unambiguously with "the appearance of the figure of Plato."[25] As he is interested more specifically in the writings of the latter insofar as they are technical traces allowing for the constitution of an intergenerational philosophical dialogue, he declares: "Thus, when you read Plato's sentences in the text *Meno*, you do not have the impression of having an approximate image of what Plato was thinking: you are in *immediate* relation with Plato's thought, and you know so intimately. You are in the *very element* of Plato's thought. [ . . . ] There can be no doubt about the signification of Plato's written statements: the discussion bears on their *meaning*—and meaning is not signification."[26]

It is odd that a philosopher so marked by the influence of Jacques Derrida would give himself over to a reflection so saturated with the metaphysics of presence. For it is as if the reading of Plato's writings is supposed to put us directly in relation with the very element of his thought and the immediate truth of the signification of his writings. We should not limit ourselves, however, to recalling the Derridean suspicion regarding univocal significations and the idea of a direct presence of truth in writing. We should go further by showing the extent to which the very notion of writing itself (*l'écriture*) is founded on a bracketing of the sociohistorical practices of the written word. The first thing to highlight in this respect is that we have nothing from the hand of Plato, and thus the idea according to which the signification of the statements attributed to the latter would be the reliable trace of his thought is unfounded: there is no proven link between "the thought" of Plato and the texts that we have at our disposal. The two principal manuscripts (Cod. Parisinus 1807 and Cod. Bodleianus 39) thanks to which we can read "Plato" date from the end of the ninth century. The corpus of the so-called father of philosophy—an expression as problematic as it is culturally specific and Eurocentric—is in reality the result of a long and complex history of canonization and codification. Moreover, the formation of this corpus depends on a hermeneutic logic dating back little more than two centuries. As I have attempted to show elsewhere, it is from within this new hermeneutic logic that one begins to become interested in the authenticity of Plato's writings, taking care to separate from them writings judged apocryphal, distinguishing between the singularity of Plato's thought and "Platonism," identifying Platonic philosophy with the thought of an individual, and basing the understanding of Plato solely on the interpretation of his writings.[27] This shows that it is not only "Plato's writing" that is a sociohistorical phenomenon through and through, but also the interpretation of Plato (and the reading proposed by Stiegler is clearly dependent upon this new hermeneutic logic). We should therefore highlight that what we call Plato's writing was a very specific practice, tightly linked to a unique cultural world, as has been clearly shown by interpreters like Eric Havelock and Jonathan Barnes (according to the latter, it is possible that Plato dictated his dialogues, perhaps to more than one scribe at a time).[28] Instead of transposing the modern practice of writing onto the entire history of this technique (or, for that matter, making writing into the vehicle for the present truth of thought), we must be very attentive to the way that technologies only have meaning in their social inscription. In short, writing, like other technologies, does not exist *in itself*; it is always part of a cultural environment, of a hermeneutic logic, and of a complex network of sociohistorical practices.

Technophobia or Technophilia

Once technology is isolated from its social inscription, one often engages in normative judgments in order to decide on its social value as a whole. Two fixed positions structure the field of possibilities: technophobia and technophilia. Intermediate and hybrid stances do not change anything with respect to the basic methodology: it is a matter of judging technology itself as a whole (even if this means dividing it between good and bad technologies). In the case of technophobia, the emphasis placed on the harmful effects of new technologies is often bolstered by a catastrophic discourse and a historical logic based on the supposed decline of humanity. The opposite position tends quite simply to invert the same schema by means of a triumphalist discourse and an evolutionary logic of history. Catastrophe or triumph, decline or progress, history can only follow the path of decadence or of evolution, as if the totality of time directed itself toward a sole and unique end. Regarding intermediate positions, there is less of a fluid trajectory than a movement in fits and starts: history continues most of the time to advance in a single direction, but with a limp.

In judging the benefits or the damaging effects of technology, two orientations are predominant. Some assert that it is technology itself that is responsible for them. Others declare that it all depends on the use one makes of it, technical tools being in effect only neutral instruments. Castoriadis perfectly described this polarity: "But we find the same thing if we consider the overall attitude toward technology: contemporary opinion, both of the general public and of experts, most often remains caught up in an antithesis between technology as a pure instrument of man (maybe wrongly used at present) and technology as an autonomous factor, a fatality or 'destiny' (whether beneficent or maleficent)."[29] Such an opposition is based in the end on the dualism of *Homo sapiens* and machine, of subject and object, of human being and world, of free action and determination. It presupposes that technology itself is an element of the world, an external determinant or a neutral object. However, technology is not simply "there" as an independent force or an instrument to use. It only exists to the extent that it is part of specific practices in a social ecology. We should therefore, as Andrew Feenberg has suggested, reject substantive theses as well as instrumentalist theses; for technology is strictly speaking "a scene of struggle."[30]

This does not mean that technologies exert no influence on practices or are not subjected to divergent uses. On the contrary, it is indeed a matter here of emphasizing the multiple consequences and the plurality of uses of technologies by breaking with the ossified opposition between human being and the world. It is not a question, however, of limiting ourselves to highlighting the multiplicity of effects and uses without assailing the conceptual system subtending the debate on technology. This implies dismantling vertical historical logic, technological essentialism, and reductive determinism with the goal of breaking once and for all with epochal thought, the monolithic conception of technology and categorical and more or less peremptory judgments that make univocal facts out of social phenomena. To put it somewhat schematically, since technology does not exist in itself, "it" is neither continuous nor discontinuous, neither autonomous nor heteronomous, neither laudable nor reprehensible.

### Digression on the Advent of Talking Pictures, or, Toward a Social Conception of Technologies

Let us pause briefly to consider a specific case that sheds light on this imbrication of technology and social practices: the so-called advent of talking pictures. Contrary to what is often claimed, this was not at all the result of an inevitable technological evolution. There had been numerous experiments with adding sound to cinema since at least those of Thomas Edison at the end of the nineteenth century: three manufacturers presented audio systems at the World's Fair of 1900 in Paris; a theater in Marseille was apparently equipped with an audio system around 1912; Gaumont filed a patent in 1918 and organized an audio projection on June 15, 1922; and so forth. The history of this technology, or rather of this diverse set of recording processes (unified after the fact under the term *talkie*), was intertwined with economic, institutional, representational, and other factors. The cost of changes, whether in production, distribution, or projection, doubtless had a significant impact on the development of talking pictures, as did the condition of the institutional structures in place (the production system, studios, the distribution system, theaters, etc.). Concerning distribution, we must not forget that the talkie signaled the end of a certain form of universal cinema insofar as the silent language of bodies was not at all limited by specific languages as in talking pictures. It also led to transformations in cinematographic representation for several reasons: technical complications linked to audio recording (which generally led to the reduction of camera movements), public enthusiasm for the talkie and hence the need to show "talking heads," the primacy of the expressivity of language over the expressivity of bodies (which had an impact on acting), and so forth. In short, "technology" was not the motor of the history of cinema, but neither was it a heteronomous element, entirely determined by external factors. The diverse processes of audio recording, unified ex post facto under the concept of the talkie, were intertwined with economic, industrial, social, and aesthetic practices, among others. Technology, far from existing "in itself," is always necessarily rooted in specific sociohistorical practices.

The case of Charlie Chaplin is quite revealing in this regard. It is known that he stalwartly resisted the talkie and developed a number of arguments against it at the end of the 1920s and the beginning of the 1930s:

> "Talkies"? You can tell 'em I loathe them.... They are spoiling the oldest art in the world—the art of pantomime. They are ruining the great beauty of silence.[31]

> Pantomime, which is the oldest of the arts, better expresses emotions than speech.[32]

> The material advantage of pantomime over speech is that it is a universal language. The Chinese children, the Japanese children, the Hindu,

the Hottentot, all understand me. I doubt whether they would understand my Chinese or my Hindustani.[33]

Despite his very harsh words regarding talking pictures, and even his assertion that "the essence of cinema is silence," we must recognize that Chaplin was not a simple technophobe.[34] His resistance to a certain form of recorded sound—he was not at all against the use of music—was precisely linked to his recognition of the fact that the technique of the talkie was bound up with specific aesthetic practices and posed considerable problems for the transcultural distribution of his art. The advent of the talking film sounded the death knell, in his view, of the art of pantomiming, of this silent and universal language of bodies, for which he had received worldwide recognition as the indisputable master. This art—the most ancient one, according to the director of *City Lights*—had the advantage of being accessible to everyone, since it did not presuppose the mastery of a specific language. It was thus the link between a specific technology and the decline of a unique artistic form, available for everyone, that was the source of his resistance to talking pictures. It was not technology itself that disturbed him, but *a* technology (talking pictures rather than sound cinema) insofar as it was bound up with an aesthetic practice and a system of distribution.

This is evidenced by his own—very belated—transition to the talkie with *The Great Dictator* (1940). He juxtaposed, in this film, the nearly absolute silence of the Jewish barber with the virulent onomatopoeia of the dictator Hynkel, which are as universally comprehensible as the screeches of animals. This is in effect an ingenious solution—even if it remains partial and provisory—to the problematic of the talkie, insofar as Chaplin was able to invent a spoken language as universal as the mute language of bodies. In doing so, he recounts at the same time the story of his own coming to speech, which is perfectly summarized at the end of the film when the Jewish barber (an avatar of Charlie) takes Hynkel's place (who had, like Hitler, "stolen" Chaplin's moustache and dominated the devices of audio broadcasting) and must indeed *give a speech*. The discussion between Schultz and the barber at this key moment obviously has a double meaning:

SCHULTZ: You must speak.
JEWISH BARBER: I can't.
SCHULTZ: You must. It's our only hope.

By finally taking the floor, the Jewish barber, as a veritable stand-in for Chaplin himself, indulges in a harangue against the mechanization of human beings. His ardent appeal to humanity is not, however, a simple condemnation of technology. On the contrary, the Jewish barber appropriates the radio (as Chaplin had taken hold of talking pictures) to struggle against all of those who make use of audiovisual devices with the goal of exploiting human beings. The act of coming to speech is thereby staged as a genuine political act of struggling for the emancipation of humanity. We thus see here another example of the way technology is always embedded, which is to say intertwined in society, in this case in political struggles concerning the broadcasting of speech.[35] Instead of inciting us to simply take a position for or against technology, the case of Chaplin invites us to consider the multiple dimensions of diverse technologies and of their social inscription by setting aside categorical judgments in favor of circumstantial decisions.

Toward a New Conception of Technologies

The act of calling into question the conceptual coordinates of a significant portion of the debate on contemporary technology by no means condemns us to abandon the question of technology and of the specificity of our historical conjuncture. On the contrary, it works to create a break, profoundly and definitively, with the structures that are largely determinative of the current controversy in order to propose a different conception of technologies. Instead of searching for the umpteenth epochal concept or entering into an ultimately tiresome debate on the continuity or discontinuity of a particular social phenomenon, it is a matter of proposing an alternative historical logic in order to think the present differently, in particular by taking into account the three dimensions of history—the vertical dimension of time, the horizontal dimension of space, and the stratigraphic dimension of the diverse practices of each space-time—so as to be able to chart the metastatic transformations of our conjuncture. At the same time, it is absolutely necessary to recognize that technology is not an isolated or isolatable fact and that it is thus neither autonomous nor heteronomous. It is always interlaced with diverse sociohistorical practices. This is to say that there is no technology in the singular. There are only embedded technologies, linked in different ways to an entire field of sociohistorical, political, economic, and cultural forces. It would perhaps be legitimate to speak, in this respect, of a *technological ecology* inasmuch as technologies constitute themselves by composing a world with an entire ensemble of practices. There would thus be something like a technological environment that is by no means external to actors but, rather, is made up of the complex intertwining of diverse activities and of their material inscriptions. In any event, it should be noted that it is not possible to judge technology as a whole from a technophile or technophobe point of view. We should rather develop circumstantial judgments that are attentive to the interweaving of technologies in other practices and to the fact that no social phenomenon has an absolutely univocal meaning. In short, the critique of the conceptual coordinates of the debate on technology, which is inscribed more generally in a counter-history of the present, aims at opening paths toward a new conception of technologies.

CHAPTER 3

# What Is the Use of Democracy?
*Urgency of an Inappropriate Question*

The Value-Concept of Democracy

It is almost universally felt that when we call a country democratic we are praising it: consequently the defenders of every kind of regime claim that it is a democracy, and fear that they might have to stop using the word if it were tied down to any one meaning.
—George Orwell

It's one of those detestable words that have more value than meaning, that sing more than they speak.
—Paul Valéry on freedom

The massive valorization of democracy in the dominant political imaginary risks preventing any in-depth questioning. For a normative or even meta-normative consensus imposes itself with such force today that it is extremely difficult to speak of democracy without presupposing its intrinsic value, or perhaps even being induced to effectively accept it as the only viable system, the political endgame, or the veritable end of history. One does not have to accept Francis Fukuyama's thesis—which is as schematic as it is problematic—in order to be taken in by the same political imaginary, as has been amply demonstrated by all of the criticisms of Fukuyama that have limited themselves to playing a positive form of democracy off against a negative form.

The first step to take consists in resisting the normative blackmail of our conjuncture by refusing to be simply for or against democracy. The normative charge of this notion tends indeed to diminish or even destroy its descriptive value. The result is, at times, a ban from the outset, in the name of a simple intellectual reflex, on all in-depth questioning and analytic investigation. This reflex is founded on a political value deemed intrinsic and—rather ironically "in a democracy"—indisputable: you are *for us or against us!*[1] This is one sign among others that democracy has come to function largely as a value-concept, an emblem of allegiance, a rallying sign, rather than as an analytic notion allowing us to distinguish between political regimes in a more or less rigorous fashion. Indeed, to the question "What does *democracy* mean today?" the obvious response in many cases is quite simply: "Whatever is approved of by the person speaking." Above all, it is a term of endorsement, if not of benediction, that often functions independently of the concrete contents of its referent.

Resistance to such blackmail is not a matter of playing facts off against norms or description against value, as if there were a clean distinction between two autonomous registers and it was simply necessary to return to a neutral depiction of the empirical givens. What are called facts and norms are interlaced and mutually implicated such that their separation can only be made heuristically by constructing conceptual abstractions. Proof of this is to be found in the fact—if I can use this term—that the appeal to a description without values is itself explicitly founded on the *value* of such a description. Speaking of normative blackmail allows us to foreground the critical threshold where certain values, which function largely as indubitable meta-values, tend to prevent from the outset forms of inquiry that one could call untimely—in particular, questions about the status of unquestioned givens in our supposed common reality, which themselves have a strong normative charge: Are we really in a democracy? Is it a good thing? Why exactly has the notion of democracy become the object of such veneration in the contemporary conjuncture? If the history of modern democracy in the Euro-American world has also been the history of the genocide of indigenous populations and of their "dreams" (according to Black Elk's powerful description),[2] of slavery and its institutional prolongations, of imperialism and colonization, of the subjugation of women and the persistence of the patriarchy, of xenophobia and the oppression of immigrants, of the exclusion of the disabled, of heteronormativity and queer- and transphobia, and of the vast and various damaging effects of capitalism including the unbridled destruction of the biosphere, then why draw the conclusion that this is the best form of government, or even the sole and unique historical possibility?[3] If one replies, very rightly, that movements proclaiming themselves to be democratic have fought body and soul against such practices and have often won, one is still forced to admit that the reverse is equally true and that this concept in struggle has frequently been pulled in the other direction, as we shall see.[4] It is therefore necessary to ask why, when references are made to the numerous stains on this history, one so often responds by invoking progress toward an idea of something *to come*, toward an immaculate notion standing above the effective history of actually existing democracy. And most of the time this happens without inquiring into the possibility of a deep complicity between this idea and the numerous forms of oppression at work in real democracy. What are the affects, so powerful yet so under-studied, that bind us implacably to this Idea, and from whence do they come?

Radical historicism is of great importance in this context, since it consists in recognizing that all of our concepts, practices, affects, and values, even those most dear to us, are historical formations. It thereby allows us to take a step back from the normative and affective pressures of contemporary reality by resituating—in this case—the cult of democracy in the long history of political cultures. In doing so, it is capable of bringing to light the historical contingency of the reigning political imaginary and, more generally, of the nearly systematic valorization of democracy in the so-called Western world (which dates back only approximately 150 years). Thus, instead of being reduced to an archeology with a purely descriptive vocation, radical historicism bears within itself a transformative power to the extent that it can lay the foundations for a historical critique by denaturalizing the normative structures and unquestioned intellectual givens of the moment. By taking a long-term perspective on "the present day" it serves, therefore, as a remedy to the usual historical myopia by bringing to the fore everything that generally remains invisible under the tyranny of the contemporary. For one only needs to go back a short while to overturn the consensus that seems to go without saying: several centuries ago, we "all" would have been absolutely in agreement and just as fiercely attached to our most fundamental and indisputable political values, but with one important difference, namely that our judgment concerning democracy would have quite simply been the opposite.

Let us therefore be very clear from the outset: the critical reflections on democracy that follow, even when severe or "savage," do not at all aim to overturn the current consensus by making us once again hostile to democracy. Nor is it a question of consigning to oblivion or condemning in advance the numerous political movements that aim at creating a more real, more radical, more substantial democracy. If it has been necessary to intervene forcefully in order to unseat common sense by questioning the supposed intrinsic value of democratic governance, this has not at all been in order to reprove all of the activists who align themselves, in specific contexts and for reasons as diverse as they are precise, with this concept in struggle. Even less so is it a question of giving up the fight by folding to the status quo, as if it had definitively recuperated this term. It would be insufficient to represent the recent history of the notion of democracy as a unilateral recuperation that has emptied it of its meaning in favor of purely ideological uses. This concept in struggle has served, without a doubt, as a banner for very diverse demands, including profound questionings of contemporary governmental systems. Thus, it is not a matter of abandoning this term to the enemy, so to speak, but rather one of radicalizing the response by breaking with the dominant historico-political imaginary, beginning with a firm resistance to its normative and affective order. This can keep us from being content from the outset with a field of possibilities delimited in advance, in such a way that we can only hope, at best, for an improvement of what is today called democracy. It is vital, moreover, to give ourselves the means to engage in the questioning of a value that is supposed to go without saying, and more generally of the very way in which we do politics and political theory. Far from surrendering, my approach consists rather, as we shall see, in trying to create a breach in the political thought of our times in order to mine beneath the formalist and abstract question of the best form of government.

The objective of this intervention is not, let it be understood, to endorse a binary, schematic normativity by simply proposing a history of democracy that would be the opposite of what is commonly assumed. On the contrary, the counter-history at stake here aims at sketching an alternative topography that approaches in a completely different manner the issue of the present by inscribing it within the long history of political cultures and by calling into question the theoretical, historiographical, and axiological frameworks subtending contemporary democratic common sense. It is a matter of etching a divide into contemporary reality, of creating a breach in the ambient political consensus, in order to forge a space of thought without the meta-normative exigencies of the moment immediately stifling all interrogation that goes against the presumed direction—and meaning—of history. This divide will also allow us to raise the very important problem of the purity of the political. As we shall see, one cannot isolate the discussion of democracy from the analysis of all of the diverse practices that animate the socioeconomic and cultural world, practices that are able to transform from top to bottom the very meaning of forms of government.

If democratophilia is particularly powerful today, this is in part because it is inscribed within a triumphalist historical logic that has, for more than thirty years, been imposing itself in the economic, political, and social realms. According to a very widespread schema of understanding, the revolutionary politics of the beginning of the twentieth century culminated in the Gulag and in various forms of totalitarianism before collapsing when faced with the rising power of what Margaret Thatcher had the audacity to call "the crusade of popular capitalism."[5] Henceforth, we have apparently been living in the era of the inevitable, as expressed in the famous slogan of the Iron Lady: TINA, or *There Is No Alternative*. The present era is supposedly the age of the end of political illusions. After the night of dreamy and utopian debauchery there purportedly follows the dawn of democratic sobriety. The failure of alternatives obliges us to face the facts, namely that democracy—working hand in hand, moreover, with so-called popular capitalism—is the only possible political system

History has subtly been converted into destiny, here, in the very era when the destinies of history—in their Marxian forms—were supposed to have been refuted once and for all. We have arrived at an epistemological utopia stretching far beyond, by towering over them, all imaginable political utopias. Indeed, we apparently know definitively today, without the least doubt, that there exists one and only one possible form of government: the one that "we" supposedly invented at the beginning of our own history. We must not overlook, then, the fact that this historical logic goes hand in hand with a geographic and cultural order that is extremely specific: it is Europe that purportedly created, at the very moment of its supposed Greek inauguration, the best possible political system.⁶ The fact that we would become aware of this today simply illustrates that the absolute knowledge of which Hegel spoke is not a thing of the past. It carries on quite well, no doubt in a form just as Eurocentric, in the era of the supposed end of metanarratives.

The question, then, that needs to be raised is whether the reference to democracy has not replaced the reference to civilization, at least in certain discourses and practices. Just like European culture, which purportedly shined as the glory of the world in the great era of colonialism, does not democracy spread itself today from its civilizational citadel with an extraordinary force of attraction? Only the most entrenched barbarians, it is said, would still resist its power of enchantment. It has therefore sometimes been necessary—as with civilization in the past—to impose it, with the help of vast and powerful military interventions, on those who are still too blind to immediately perceive its benefits. Has democracy not thereby come to play approximately the same role for globalized neoliberal capitalism as civilization once played for the colonial endeavors of imperialist capitalism? "With the debacle of bureaucratic despotism and of actually non-existent socialism," wrote Daniel Bensaïd, "the floating signifier of democracy became a synonym for the victorious West, the triumphant United States of America, the free market, and undistorted competition."⁷ Today, has not the civilizing mission become decidedly "democratic"? If we believe a visionary like Arthur Rimbaud, capitalist imperialism had already aligned itself under the banner of democracy for some time. His poem "Democracy," written at the start of the bloody interventions of the Third Republic, speaks volumes on the troubling future of this banner-concept:

> The flag moves through a disgusting landscape, and our patois drowns out the drum.
> In the interior, we shall fuel the most cynical prostitution. We shall massacre every revolt which makes sense.
> Hello, sodden lands of spices!—serving the most monstrous industrial or military exploitation.
> Goodbye to here, anywhere will do. Conscripts of goodwill, our philosophy will be ferocious; knowing nothing about science, everything about comforts; the world and its ways can go hang. This is the true way forward. Quick march!⁸

Without condemning it in advance, I will open here an untimely interrogation into democracy that has no a priori limit and that does not therefore accept to subjugate thought and action to the normative policing of the common sense of the moment, this ferocious philosophy of contemporary reality.

Democratic Theodicy

It was absurd to die for Danzig; it will be reasonable to die for democracy.
At least, that's what they repeat to us every day.
—Jean-Paul Sartre

To wish to arrest democracy would then seem tantamount to a struggle against God Himself.
—Alexis de Tocqueville

The triumphalist historical logic of democracy constitutes a veritable theodicy, and it remains generally impermeable to the "facts" able to oppose it. Just as with the historical logic of vulgar Marxism (which should not of course be confused with Marx's writings), of which it is a clandestine echo, setbacks and delays do nothing but confirm the direction of history and above all the necessity that history should continue to follow its path and progress. Belief in the end of history, be it democratic or Marxist, surpasses the simple world of facts. It is surely for this reason that an author like Fukuyama, through a stupendous recuperation, took ownership of what he identifies as Hegelian-Marxist (and above all idealist) historiography. He declares in no uncertain terms and on several occasions that it is the *idea* of democracy, and by no means its material practice, that guides the necessary development of history: "The fact that there will be setbacks and disappointments in the process of democratization, or that not every market economy will prosper, should not distract us from the larger pattern that is emerging in world history [ . . . ]. What is emerging victorious, in other words, is not so much liberal practice, as the liberal *idea*. That is to say, for a very large part of the world, there is now no ideology with pretensions to universality that is in a position to challenge liberal democracy, and no universal principle of legitimacy other than the sovereignty of the people."[9] By "sovereignty of the people," we should note that Fukuyama means nothing more than the right to vote and to participate in politics: "Democracy [ . . . ] is the right held universally by all citizens to have a share of political power, that is, the right of all citizens to vote and participate in politics."[10]

Here it is necessary to bring to the fore a major and highly revealing difference, at least in the common sense pervading our historical conjuncture, between the idea of communism and that of democracy. It is sometimes said of communism that it was, in fact, a good idea on paper, but that the reality was a veritable catastrophe. One thereby highlights a discrepancy between political theory and historical reality by insisting on the fact that the idea of communism is perhaps quite simply not realizable. One sometimes adds for good measure that it was precisely faith in the communist idea—a faith that lies beyond the reach of the manifest evidence of concrete experience—that led to the totalitarian turn of actually existing communism. Yet on the other hand, when one speaks of democracy, this type of criticism is no longer operative. One frequently admits that contemporary institutions are not perfect, that actually existing democracy has insufficiencies, that there is still progress to be made, that there is a democratic deficit, or that democracy quite simply remains to come. But despite all the setbacks and all the limitations of contemporary practices, people shout themselves hoarse proclaiming that it is a good idea, or even that it is the sole and unique Idea. In one instance, reality takes precedence over the idea; in the other, the idea gains the upper hand over reality. At base, the same operation is at work, which is a comparison between an ideal system and its historical institution. Yet a revealing discrepancy manifests itself in the criteria of evaluation. In the case of communism, history is capable of refuting the idea, whereas for democracy the idea transcends historical reality and orients it toward something that is perhaps always to come. Whatever the case may be, it is impossible to call into question the democratic idea, for it hovers well above concrete practices. Towering over the real, democratic discourse thereby functions as a pseudo-science, which is to say a discourse that is beyond the reach of material refutations. Illustrating another surreptitious recuperation of vulgar Marxism, faith in the idea—this time democratic—can never be refuted by experience. If this sort of belief was what sustained the misdeeds of Soviet bureaucracy, should not one expect that the liberal recuperation would come full circle and that the icon of democracy would come to allow innumerable "anti-democratic abuses," and even the development of what Sheldon Wolin has called "inverted totalitarianism" (see below)?

In order to take a step back from the consensual faith in democracy, it does not suffice, then, to appeal to "the facts" (a term that is problematic enough, for that matter, to require its own investigation). It is necessary to attack the historical order that produces *givens*—that is, seemingly indubitable, unquestioned realities. It is in this sense that a counter-history does not play facts off against facts but works to construe entirely differently what presents itself as a set of historical positivities. What is at stake, in truth, is a reconfiguration of the regime of historical perception, which is also a regime of thinking.

At the heart of the triumphalist historical logic of democratic theodicy is the Whig conception of history and the idea of a presumed progress toward a telos. This notion generally depends on selective historicism insofar as it tends to presuppose an extra-historical object of analysis and system of values. To judge that progress exists, one acts as if there were something comparable that does not change between the two historical moments in question. This is to say that progress in this sense presupposes the progress of *something* that remains stable enough to be compared across time. It is also founded on a system of values largely independent of historical evolution, for if the criteria of judgment were to change with history, then one could not offer a definitive judgment on progress. Let us note, finally, that the notion of progress tends to base itself on a vertical logic of history by bracketing the horizontal dimension of space and the stratigraphic dimension of diverse social practices. Taking into account geographic and social space would do nothing other than disrupt historical linearity by dispersing it into constellations as diverse as they are specific. In the traditional thinking of progress—and the same goes for that of decline—one compares two phenomena deemed homologous on a vertical axis of chronology with regard to a supposedly universal, or at least trans-epochal, criterion.

Without lingering on the emergence of the modern notion of progress, which would show that it is historically constructed, the following analysis aims to demonstrate that the massive valorization of democracy in the so-called Western world is a phenomenon of recent date and that our concept and practice of democracy are very far from being trans-historical.

There is not a unique democratic principle for the entire history of humanity. There are diverse practices qualified as *democratic* and highly variable systems of values. Furthermore, the four phases of the history of "democracy" in the "West" sketched out below must absolutely be resituated in socio-geographic space by way of a detailed analysis of diverse theoretico-practical constellations. It is necessary, moreover, to recall that social phenomena such as politics are necessarily plurivocal and have variable effects according to the complex topography of society. This or that "advance" at a certain level for a given sector of society can in every way constitute a "reversion" at other levels or for other parts of society (or at other moments). Politics as a social phenomenon is never univocal, and it is thus impossible to judge political developments as a whole according to the models of progress or decline. There are transformations with variable consequences that are themselves judged on the basis of systems of values inscribed in specific sociohistorical milieus (there is no extra-historical system of values allowing us to make a definitive judgment regarding progress or decline).

As for the supposed arrival at the end of history, it is not solely a matter of an assessment founded on a highly problematic historical logic, inherited in a contradictory and ironic fashion from vulgar Marxism. Rather, such an affirmation purports to have access to the *epistēmē* of politics, as if there were an ultimate and definitive plan for the organization of human communities. The act of dismantling this powerful historical logic and this claim to *epistēmē* constitutes an important step in retaking control of politics and of history. For if there is no end of history, if it is never closed, this is precisely because it incessantly makes and remakes itself. The only utopia that exists is not situated at the end of history but *in* history, in the immanent transformation of societies.

A Brief Intransitive History of Democracy

Until the twentieth century, most of the world proclaimed the superiority of
nondemocratic systems both in theory and in practice.
—Robert A. Dahl

Democracy as such does not exist.[11] There are only diverse sociohistorical practices qualified as *democratic* from specific points of view. And the label *democratic* has radically changed its meaning over the course of history and in different cultural matrices. Instead of accepting as such the diverse schematizations of the history of democracy's ascent to power—or even apotheosis—and rather than admitting without discussion the retroactive history that surreptitiously projects "our" democracy onto historical scenes where it was not at all operative, we should take things the other way around by sketching the broad lines of an intransitive history of so-called democracy. By intransitive history I mean a history that does not presuppose the existence of a natural object, such as Democracy, which would transcend history while simultaneously unifying it. Radical historicism requires that we resituate our own concepts in the flux of time and in geographic variability by proceeding from the start with an analytic of practices.

In what follows I propose, therefore, to sketch in broad outline four phases of "democracy" with the aim of laying the groundwork for an intransitive history of political cultures. I speak of *phases* instead of *epochs* because history is not divided by neat temporal caesuras but rather distributes itself in the three dimensions already invoked: the vertical dimension of time, the horizontal dimension of space, and the stratigraphic dimension of the social world. Whereas the notion of an epoch can be useful for referring in purely heuristic fashion to the temporal dimension of history, it has often had as a consequence the more or less total exclusion of the other two dimensions of history. The concept of a phase has the distinct advantage of foregrounding how historical phenomena always distribute themselves in a specific way in geographic and social space. In sketching the general outline of four phases of democratic practices, I would thus like to insist on the specificity of their chronological, geographic, and social distribution. It is precisely for this reason that the transitions between phases take the form of historical metastases rather than events or clean ruptures. The notion of event can be useful for speaking very schematically about a more or less rapid transformation. However, it tends to obscure the ways in which historical change implies a transformation that spreads out in space and over different levels of society.

It is necessary to insist on the geographic and cultural stakes of this history, since the reigning historico-political imaginary has so forcefully associated the notion of democracy with that of the West that they have become practically indiscernible. Since their common birth in ancient Greece—this supposed cradle of an entire civilization and tradition of thought—it is as if they have undergone a more or less identical development and unfolding inasmuch as democracy is supposedly the Western form of government par excellence. Yet democracy—one could say just as much of the West and also, for that matter, of philosophy—was not truly born in Greece. This is for a very simple reason: social practices are not born in the way that human beings purportedly are. Contrary to what the ontogenetic conception of history suggests, they do not simply appear as well-delimited entities but emerge metastatically via struggles and negotiations between a multiplicity of forces of action (which are not necessarily limited to a sole cultural zone or a single historical period). The fabrication of an origin narrative and above all of a retroactive eschatological history projecting practices and notions from the end of history—in the banal sense of the term—back onto distant historico-cultural conjunctures results in the obfuscation of these conjunctures beneath monolithic concepts that have come from elsewhere (which constitutes a veritable historical and intellectual colonization). In the terms of ontogenetic historiography, one could say, indeed, that the fashioning of such a narrative resembles in many ways the insolent act of a presumptuous child expressing a desire to choose its parents. Yet if one knows full well that such a thing is impossible in the personal realm, at least in our conjuncture, it is even more illusory at the sociohistorical level, since there is always and inevitably a plurality of parents. It is not only that one does not choose one's origins; it is, more profoundly, that there exists such a proliferation of complex and interlaced provenances that the origin is lacking. This is why it is presumed necessary to create it after the fact, to attempt to secure an identity—such as that of Western-democratic civilization *as such*—which does not exist in itself. According to David Graeber, "The notion that democracy was a distinctly 'Western' ideal only came [ . . . late]. For most of the nineteenth century, when Europeans defined themselves against 'the East' or 'the Orient,' they did so precisely as 'Europeans,' not 'Westerners.' With few exceptions, 'the West' referred to the Americas. It was only in the 1890s, when Europeans began to see the United States as part of the same, coequal civilization, that many started using the term in its current sense."[12]

If the intransitive history sketched below vaguely follows the trajectory of the triumphalist history of Democracy, from its alleged Greek birth to its Euro-American—and above all Anglo-American—apotheosis, this is not at all in order to lend credence to this teleological history. On the contrary, it is instead a matter of dissecting and dismantling it from the inside, so to speak, by calling into question the transhistorical consistency of democratic practices and the homogeneity, even in a restricted sense, of supposed Western democratic culture. On this point, Partha Chatterjee writes: "[It] is not as though, irrespective of the imperfections of Western democracies, the normative model itself remains universally valid and should be regarded as a beacon for aspiring democrats around the world. Rather, the problem is that the experience of postcolonial democracy is showing every day that those norms themselves must be rethought."[13] In the context of the decolonial struggles in North Africa, Frantz Fanon declared: "For us Algerians, the triumph of democracy does not depend solely on the Western world since it is actually this same Western world that challenges its values."[14]

In order to complete this brief history, it would be necessary to add an analysis of what one could call, very schematically, non-Western democratic practices. On this topic, I refer the reader to the important works by Benjamin Isakhan, Stephen Stockwell, Amartya Sen, and others who have inquired into the democratic practices that preceded Athenian democracy or took place in very different cultural contexts.[15] Without taking a position on the various arguments advanced by these authors (to which I will return shortly), it is imperative to ask ourselves whether it is probable that democracy is the privilege of the West, since this category is itself a cultural and historical fabrication without neat or watertight borders. Properly speaking, the West does not exist *in itself*; it only exists *for itself* and *for others* to the extent that it is something of a social assemblage, the meaning of which remains contestable and contested. By calling into question the supposed essence of the West, it is certainly very important to look elsewhere. And the writings cited above offer numerous interesting examples of "democratic" practices having emerged a bit all over the world and throughout history. While insisting on the fundamental importance of these works and of their calling into question of the purely Western model of the history of democracy, it is also necessary to point out a risk (I insist on this term). For they often begin from the postulate that democracy is a good in itself, only to then excavate examples of the contemporary West's prized and self-proclaimed value outside its own borders, with the goal of showing, like a good cultural archaeologist, that the rest of the world is not so backward. In extreme cases, it is somewhat as if one were to say, "You know, they are respectable, these people, because they have the same values as us!" From the privilege of the West, democracy comes to transform itself into the potential privilege of all cultures, of all historical periods, even of humanity as a whole.[16] Yet the fundamental values remain the same, and one acts as if there were in effect a sole and unique concept capable of overseeing an entire complex of very specific cultural practices. It is revealing, in this respect, that the authors cited inquire very little into the specificity of the endogenous notions and terms used to describe the practices they baptize with the name of democracy (thanks to an extension of the notion, which is at times considerable). In truth, this global history of the democratization of democracy is also a symptom of our historical conjuncture, and of the transformation of the notion of democracy into a value-concept: democracy, rather than being an analytic concept for describing a specific practice, has largely become a term of approval, even of benediction, for making reference to something relatively abstract and general—like "the good"—that one venerates, independently of its precise content. Yet if democracy is not the sole privilege of the West, it is not because it is a good in itself whose traces can be found elsewhere by conforming cultural archeologists, especially if it is given a large, or even elastic, definition. Rather, it is that democracy in itself does not exist, and that the values attached to this concept in struggle, to this floating signifier, have varied considerably across cultural conjunctures.

## *DĒMOKRATIA*

The traditional story of the emergence of democracy resembles in many respects the birth of Athena. Just as the goddess of war and wisdom is supposed to have sprung forth fully formed from Zeus's head, so too is democracy as such supposed to have suddenly leapt out from the mind of the citizens of Athens. Yet, given that history always involves a multiplicity of actors, its developments remain irreducible to the ontogenetic model of individual life. It knows no birth, properly speaking, and certainly not a nearly immaculate inception of this kind. It is thus better to speak of *emergence* rather than *birth*, for there exists a multidimensional process that is not necessarily unified or homogeneous. A historical emergence thus functions as a metastasis without a priori unity, or a reconfiguration that distributes itself unequally in time, space, and the social conjuncture. To say that the Greeks, and moreover the Athenians, invented or gave birth to democracy is to construct a retroactive origin narrative founded on an ontogenetic historiography that ignores the social dimension of the metastatic formation of political practices.[17] Such a narrative takes shape above all in the modern age, notably due to the "Western" rediscovery of ancient Greece and of its relatively expansive and accessible archive (which is unfortunately lacking for numerous other cultures that could themselves have been equally, or even more, "democratic"). This narrative filters out the complexity of social-historical developments in order to extract a simple plotline by which it can depict the West as marching from a single origin to a unique end point. The political stakes of this tightrope walk of history are obviously considerable, for the acrobat of civilization purports to be able to rise far above the crowd of cultures deemed less developed.

Some authors have attempted to open up the field of analysis by examining, as much as one can, the political practices foreshadowing those of ancient Greece, whether it be the so-called primitive democracy of the ancient Middle East or the popular government of Phoenicia.[18] Let us, however, take the traditional starting point with the precise aim of foregrounding several elements that are often obscured or set aside. "The Greeks gave us the word," recounts Anthony H. Birch, "but did not provide us with a model. The assumptions and practices of the Greeks were very different from those of modern democrats."[19] Without pretending to be exhaustive, for we must recognize the limits of our historical knowledge due in particular to incomplete records, let us note that Athenian democracy was a direct democracy and that the Assembly was open to all of the citizens.[20] It was limited to a city of about 42,000 or 43,000 citizens, among a population of approximately 250,000 people.[21] There was no state as an autonomous apparatus, distinct from the collectivity or from what Aristotle called the political association (*koinōnia politikē*), which meant the community of citizens. There existed, for that matter, a rigid and naturalized distinction between citizens (Greek men) and non-citizens (women, children, slaves, metics), and the latter, which constituted by far the majority of the population, did not participate in politics. Around 17 percent of the inhabitants of Athens were citizens, of which up to 6,000—or only 2.4 percent of the population—could be present at the Assembly.[22] Furthermore, there were no professional politicians in the modern sense of the term, nor political parties. The individualism of modern democracy was also lacking, as well as liberalism, and political activity was very much centered on the collectivity or the group of men formed by *paideia*. Religion and mythology played an absolutely central role. The concept of democracy was, moreover, a new idea, apparently an offshoot of the notion of isonomia, and even a word of scorn invented precisely to condemn the partisans of the *dēmos* (which suggests, for that matter, that the axiological tenor of the term is nothing new).[23] Finally, a properly universal dimension was lacking from political activity, and the geographic scale was more restricted.[24] On all these points, the concept and the practice of Athenian democracy clearly distinguished themselves from the modern notion and practice.

Additionally, unlike with the contemporary cult of democracy, the majority of Greek thinkers held democracy in low regard. "In antiquity," recalls the historian Moses Finley, "intellectuals in the overwhelming majority disapproved of popular government [ . . . ]. Today, their counterparts, especially but not only in the West, are agreed, in probably the same overwhelming majority, that democracy is the best form of government, the best known and the best imaginable."[25]

### YEARS IN THE DESERT

The reference to democracy as a current practice largely disappeared between the end of Antiquity and the seventeenth and, above all, eighteenth centuries: "One may say that during the Middle Ages and even until the 17th century, the word 'democracy' remained a scholarly word, the usage of which was generally restricted to designating a very specific form of ancient constitution."[26] The term, when it was employed, made reference primarily to a practice that was no longer operative. "[For] a long time," writes Pierre Rosanvallon, "the word 'democracy' was used only to designate an obsolete type of political system. In the 18th century, it was employed exclusively in reference to the ancient world."[27] There may potentially be some exceptions to point out, such as the *Landsgemeinde* of the rural cantons in Switzerland, but the general tendency of this phase does not appear to be up for debate, especially with respect to the use of the term *democracy*.[28]

To illustrate this general disappearance, which would be followed by a timid return toward the end of this phase, let us highlight the striking case of John Locke (1632–1704). Although he is frequently identified as one of the founders of modern democracy, only a small handful of references to democracy can be found in his entire corpus. In one of the principal passages where he evokes it, he does so precisely in order to distinguish it from the *commonwealth*, which constitutes his true object of analysis: "By *Common-wealth*, I must be understood all along to mean, not a democracy, or any form of government, but *any Independent Community*, which the *Latines* signified by the word *Civitas*, to which the word which best answers in our language, is *Common-wealth*."[29] We should note in passing that the authors of "The Fundamental Constitutions of Carolina" call for democracy to be avoided in a paragraph written in the handwriting of Locke, who was one of its authors.[30] Contrary, then, to what is sometimes claimed, there is no argued defense or theory of democracy in Locke.[31]

The same goes for the English activists of the seventeenth century known under the injurious name of Levellers. They certainly defended popular sovereignty, religious tolerance, the existence of natural rights, and the contractual foundation of political authority. They even called, in some of their texts, for economic justice by relying on an idea of natural equality and human interdependence.[32] Yet they did not at all lay claim to democracy. And this was for good reason: the word had negative connotations and functioned primarily as a term of abuse.[33] Certain commentators have nevertheless wanted to see in them a kind of democratic spirit before its time. However, one must be very careful with this type of argument, which risks putting charged and anachronistic words into the mouths of our ancestors. The problem is not simply the historical reconfiguration that inevitably results from a lexical change. It is the construction of a retro-progressive history—in the sense that it is at once retroactive and progressive—of the great march of liberal democracy, burying unceremoniously everything that would render more complex such a linear narrative of ascent.

If one is looking for a genuine claim to democracy in its own proper name, several important traces are to be found in the seventeenth century.

The constitution of Rhode Island, signed in 1641, appears to be one of the first democratic documents in the Euro-American world, for the state in question was founded as "a Democracy or popular government."[34] The intellectual milieu of Baruch Spinoza (1632–77) in Holland also evinces positive references to democracy. Proposing to define it as "a united gathering of people which collectively has the sovereign right to do all that it has the power to do [*caetus universus hominum, qui collegialiter summum jus ad omnia, quae potest, habet*]," the author of the *Theological-Political Treatise* explicitly praised this form of government, which he described as the most natural and the most apt to preserve human freedom.[35] He largely followed the work of Johan de la Court, according to Jonathan Israel's meticulous analysis. The latter has masterfully questioned the preponderance of the Anglo-American republican tradition in histories of democracy, which has resulted in the marginalization or overshadowing of the very important work of authors such as Spinoza, de la Court, van den Enden, Koerbagh, Walten, and van Leenhof.[36] In this network of thinkers, one finds several of the first traces of a modern, explicit, and argued defense of democracy as the best form of government. Nevertheless, this still remains extremely exceptional at this time.

POWER OF THE RABBLE

When the term and the concept of democracy slowly began to be used more widely starting with the Enlightenment or a bit before, they generally expressed an unfavorable judgment. As Raymond Williams reminds us, the term *democracy* meant more or less mob rule and had rather negative connotations.[37] According to Bertlinde Laniel, this image of democracy persisted: "During at least the first quarter of the 19th century, these words [*democracy* and *democratic*] still smelled of sulfur, revolution, and anarchy, and their usage by numerous Americans still implied a strong disapproval. In Europe, it was necessary to await even the 20th century before the word 'democratic,' for example, would become respectable, expressing in general a favorable judgment."[38]

Let us look at some examples of authors often identified today as thinkers of the democratic tradition, if not as the veritable founding fathers of modern democracy. Jean-Jacques Rousseau (1712–78), like Montesquieu (1689–1755) before him, was not a simple defender of democracy. The latter wrote: "The principle of democracy is corrupted not only when the spirit of equality is lost but also when the spirit of extreme equality is taken up and each one wants to be the equal of those chosen to command."[39] The true spirit of equality is thus neatly distinguished for him from the spirit of extreme equality.[40] This is because the representatives, contrary to the people, are capable of deliberating on political and social affairs: "The great advantage of representatives is that they are able to discuss public business. The people are not at all appropriate for such discussions; this forms one of the great drawbacks of democracy."[41] In the end, then, Montesquieu presupposes the existence of a social hierarchy that must be maintained in the organization of government: "In a state there are always some people who are distinguished by birth, wealth, or honors; but if they were mixed among the people and if they had only one voice like the others, the common liberty would be their enslavement and they would have no interest in defending it, because most of the resolutions would be against them."[42] Rousseau, for his part, affirmed that the best form of government always depends on the situation and that there is no general rule in this domain. In the strict sense of the term, he even declared that democracy has never existed and will never exist. This is because "it is contrary to the natural order that the majority govern and the minority is governed. It is unimaginable that the people would remain constantly assembled to handle public affairs; and it is readily apparent that it could not establish commissions for this purpose without changing the form of administration."[43] He adds, for good measure, that "no government is so subject to civil wars and internal agitations as a democratic or popular one."[44] It is true that he appears to promote democratic government when he asserts: "Were there a people of gods, it would govern itself democratically."[45] However, he remains very firm in adding: "So perfect a government is not suited to men."[46] This being said, he does not have a homogeneous corpus (which can also be said of the other authors cited), and he asserts, for example, in the dedication to *Discourse on the Origin of Inequality*, that he would have liked to have been born "under a democratic government, wisely tempered."[47] He specifies, however, what he means by "wisely tempered" by writing: "I would have fled, as necessarily ill-governed, a republic where the people, believing it could get along without its magistrates or permit them but a precarious authority, would imprudently have held on to the administration of civil affairs and the execution of its own laws. Such must have been the rude constitution of the first governments immediately emerging from the state of nature, and such too was one of the vices which ruined the republic of Athens."[48]

David Hume (1711–76) evinced democratic leanings insofar as he recognized the possibility of a "pure republic" in small societies, but he immediately added that we should instead rest content "to cherish and improve our ancient government as much as possible, without encouraging a passion for such dangerous novelties."[49] Even though Giambattista Vico (1668–1744) speaks of popular republics (*repubbliche popolari*) rather than of democracies, he also established a parallel—as did many others at the time—between popular government and anarchy by explaining that popular republics without curbs "are in fact the worst form of tyranny, since there are as many tyrants as there are bold and dissolute persons in the cities."[50]

Immanuel Kant (1724–1804), for his part, formulated a trenchant critique of democracy in "Toward Perpetual Peace." He identified three forms of sovereignty (autocracy, aristocracy, democracy), while juxtaposing them to two forms of government: the republican, founded on the principle of the separation of executive and legislative power, and despotism, which ignores such a principle. On the basis of these distinctions, Kant drew the following conclusion concerning democracy: "Among the three forms of state, democracy is, according to the proper sense of the term, necessarily a form of despotism, because it establishes an executive power whereby 'all' make decisions over, and if necessary, against one (who therefore does not agree). Thus 'all' who are not actually all make decisions, which means that the general will stands in contradiction with itself and with freedom."[51] It is possible, in his view, to combine the other forms of sovereignty with republicanism, and it happens that monarchy lends itself best to a republican constitution. It suffices to recall the first definitive article with a view to perpetual peace ("The Civil Constitution of Every State Shall Be Republican") in order to see the extent to which democracy is, for Kant, the form of sovereignty that is the least conducive to perpetual peace.[52]

Such distrust regarding democracy was also very widespread in the United States in the era of the supposed "Founding Fathers." Ralph Ketcham perfectly summarized this situation by writing that "virtually all shades of opinion reviled monarchy and democracy, and, publicly at least, supported republicanism."⁵³ In effect, the distinction between democratic government and republican government was of the utmost importance (even if there were semantic variations), and politicians such as James Madison condemned the error consisting in confounding "a republic with a democracy."⁵⁴ He opposed, for his part, the qualities of republics, founded on representation and better adapted to large states, to the flaws of democracies, which are incapable of stretching across vast territories or of protecting themselves against pernicious factions.⁵⁵ In a similar fashion, Alexander Hamilton called for the unification of the states into a "confederate republic" rather than into a democracy, which he described as being unstable and imprudent.⁵⁶ William Cobbett, the editor of a pro-Federalist paper, went further still by expressing himself with remarkable candor: "O base democracy! Why, it is absolutely worse than street-sweepings, or the filth of the common sewers."⁵⁷ Yet it is perhaps John Adams who, better than anyone, lucidly summarized the dangers of democracy in the eyes of the most powerful statesmen. For he feared that the majority, who were very poor, would wish to redistribute goods and establish material equality.⁵⁸ He wrote, for instance:

> But if that is the best form of government, where governors are least exposed to the baits and snares of luxury, the government our author [Nedham] contends for is the worst of all possible forms. There is, there can be no form in which the governors are more exposed to the baits and snares of luxury as in a simple democracy. In proportion as a government is democratical, in a degree beyond a proportional prevalence of monarchy and aristocracy, the wealth, means, and opportunities being the same, does luxury prevail. Its progress is instantaneous. There can be no subordination. One citizen cannot bear that another should live better than himself; a universal emulation in luxury instantly commences [ . . . ]. Every man will do as he pleases, no sumptuary law will be obeyed; every prohibition or impost will be eluded; no man will dare to propose a law by which the pleasures of the liberty of the citizen shall be restrained. A more unfortunate argument for a simple democracy could not have been thought of.⁵⁹

When eminent members of the landowning class gathered in Philadelphia in 1787 to draw up a federal constitution, Edmund Randolph set the tone for the discussion by identifying the principal problem with the constitutions of the states: "Our chief danger arises from the democratic parts of our constitutions. It is a maxim which I hold incontrovertible, that the powers of government exercised by the people swallows up the other branches. None of the constitutions have provided sufficient checks against the democracy."[60] Among the numerous echoes of this initial clarion call present in the subsequent debate, I will limit myself to indicating but two of them: Roger Sherman proclaimed that "the people should have as little to do as may be about the Government"; and Elbridge Gerry added, "The evils we experience flow from the excess of democracy."[61]

Anti-democratic republicans or Federalists won the political battle against the anti-Federalists and established a republic opposed to democracy.[62] The U.S. Constitution adheres to this general principle by guaranteeing to each state a republican form of government (section 4, article IV). It never declares at any point, of course, that the United States will be a democracy, and it does not even guarantee the right to vote. Although the Constitutional Convention did not follow Hamilton's suggestion of naming a president and a Senate for life, "neither did it provide for popular elections," as Howard Zinn rightly reminds us, "except in the case of the House of Representatives, where the qualifications were set by the state legislatures (which required property-holding for voting in almost all the states), and excluded women, Indians, slaves. The Constitution provided for Senators to be elected by the state legislators, for the President to be elected by electors chosen by the state legislators, and for the Supreme Court to be appointed by the President."[63]

It is thus not in the least surprising that George Mason described the new constitution as the "most daring attempt to establish a despotic aristocracy among freemen, that the world has ever witnessed."[64] John DeWitt went further still in affirming that the new federal government "will degenerate to a complete Aristocracy [ ... ]. It can be said to be nothing less than a hasty stride to Universal Empire in this Western World."[65] For our present investigation, it was perhaps Patrick Henry who provided the most concise summary of the founding of the United States of America in his arguments against the new constitution: "It is not a democracy."[66] In the same enflamed speech before the Virginia Ratifying Convention, he bluntly juxtaposed the signing of this non-democratic constitution with the recent emancipation from England: "Here is a revolution as radical as that which separated us from Great Britain."[67]

## DEMOCRATOPHILIA

The last phase in this intransitive history of democracy is that of an unprecedented valorization. There were already several traces of this reversal of opinion in individuals as different as Thomas Paine (1737–1809), Thomas Tudor Tucker (1745–1828), Maximilien de Robespierre (1758–94), and Gracchus Babeuf (1760–97), not to mention several more or less radical authors of the seventeenth century. In *Rights of Man*, for instance, Paine described the American system of government as "representation ingrafted upon democracy."[68] With respect to Thomas Tucker and Robespierre, I refer the reader to Francis Dupuis-Déri's probing analysis, whose conclusion regarding the latter is relatively revealing: "Robespierre thus reappropriated the word 'democracy' and gave it a positive meaning in order to increase the popular legitimacy of his policies and of his own power, which were however increasingly dictatorial and bloody. Robespierre would even come to claim that the Terror results from the principles of 'democracy.' Despite his principled declarations in favor of democracy, Robespierre was not for all that a partisan of this regime."[69] Babeuf, by contrast, overtly declared himself to be for "pure democracy, equality without blemish and without reserve."[70]

It was not until the 1820s, and above all the 1830s, that this reversal of opinion began to spread. In the United States, this started around the era of Andrew Jackson, the first "democratic" president and the symbol of the average American (who put an end to the long reign of patricians from Virginia and Massachusetts). "It was between 1830 and 1850," writes David Graeber in a work that relies on the meticulous research by Bertlinde Laniel and others, "that politicians in the United States and France began to identify themselves as democrats and to use *democracy* to designate the electoral regime, even though no constitutional change or transformation of the decision-making process warranted this change in name."[71] Francis Dupuis-Déri, for his part, emphasizes the way in which this reversal of opinion was linked, at least in certain contexts, to a major redefinition of the term *democracy*: "It no longer makes reference to the people assembled to freely deliberate but designates on the contrary the liberal electoral regime, up to then named 'republic.'"[72] As he has shown in detail, there was a major, strategic mobilization of the term *democracy* by the men in power, if not a veritable political commercialization or publicity campaign, aiming to convince the people to adhere to and vote for elitist republics, without however changing their oligarchic structure. By imposing a more and more positive connotation on this term, particularly with the expansion of the right to vote, a new image was given to an old situation. This does not mean that everyone was duped. Indeed, Auguste Blanqui exclaimed: "Beware of words lacking definition; this is the favorite instrument of schemers. [ . . . ] Everyone purports to be a *democrat*, above all the aristocrats."[73]

Pierre Rosanvallon rightly recalls that democracy was not one of the keywords of the French Revolution: "When moderates like Antoine Barnave or the Abbé Sieyès spoke of the regime that they considered ideal, they referred to it as 'representative government.' On the other side, radicals like those who clustered around the Cordeliers group mobilized to defend the key concept of 'popular sovereignty.'"[74] He situates the semantic shift in French in the 1830s while specifying: "Indeed, it was not until 1848 that the word 'democracy' really imposed itself in political discourse in France."[75] It is revealing from this point of view that Alexis de Tocqueville (1805–59) published the first volume of his celebrated work *Democracy in America* in 1835. He formulated, in particular, what is doubtless one of the first versions of the history of the progressive and inevitable march of democracy in the Christian world (the only one that mattered), which is not at all unrelated to more contemporary versions, including secular ones: "Everywhere we have seen the various aspects of the life of peoples come to favor democracy; all men have aided it by their efforts [, . . . ] all have been driven in various ways down the same path. All have labored in common, some in spite of themselves and some without knowing it; all have been blind instruments in the hands of God. The gradual development of equality is a providential fact [ . . . ]: it is universal, it is durable, it constantly eludes human power, and all events as well as all men contribute to its development."[76]

Kristin Ross has proposed an instructive analysis of the denotative and connotative transformation of the term *democracy*, punctuated by two key moments. Starting from an insightful declaration by Auguste Blanqui, who affirmed in 1852 that the term *democrat* was a word with "a rubbery nature," she writes: "Up until then the word had largely retained its revolutionary 1789 heritage; *democrat* was the label, for example, of many far-left organizations in the 1830s and 1840s. But during the Second Empire the Imperial Regime had effectively appropriated the term for itself, for the most part successfully, by opposing what it called real 'democracy' to the bourgeois 'party of order.' "[77] She then addresses the poems of Arthur Rimbaud in the period of the Commune: "The resonance of democracy registered by Rimbaud was definitively changed, not merely diluted but filled with an alien content, as the very groups who feared it at the beginning of the century begin to embrace it at the century's end. As in Rimbaud's poem, democracy becomes a banner, a slogan, a proof of being civilized as well as the vital supplement, the ideal fig leaf, to the civilized and civilizing West. The State, in the name of representative democracy, inaugurates a history of class massacre, within Europe in the form of the Commune and beyond, in the colonial domains."[78]

This is obviously not a simple linear history, and there are significant variations, as with all of the phases of this intransitive history of democracy.[79] We could invoke, in this regard, other reference points, as for example that of the poet Walt Whitman (1819–92), who presented himself at the beginning of *Leaves of Grass* as the bard of "athletic Democracy" in America.[80] For him, democracy was neither a word with a rubbery nature nor, properly speaking, a banner. It is true that his book *Democratic Perspectives* (1871) sings the praises of the American Republic as being open to all, lauds capitalist expansion, supports the "manifest destiny" of the United States, speaks sometimes of a supposed superiority of the American race, denigrates the miserable and ignorant at the same moment that he celebrates the people, and intermixes his criticisms of the social-moral failures of democracy with an irrepressible admiration for the material and financial advances of the Unites States. In all of this, he obviously is not far from the idea of democracy as a banner for the civilization of the "New World." Yet his principal argument in this work consists in saying that democracy in America remains stuck in the material domain and therefore needs a spiritual elevation. Literature, this unparalleled force of collective and national education, is the privileged vehicle for this much-needed transformation. It is in this way that he describes America as being between two revolutions: the material revolution, which is behind it, and the spiritual revolution that is still to come.[81] He thus appeals to the need for a new American literature that, by breaking with the aristocratic principles of previous writers and literati in the name of a poetry of the people, will nourish a renewal of the nation's soul by forming new citizens by means of unprecedented models of life. Speaking of the people, of the worker, of the peasant, of woman equal to man, this democratic literature of all people will allow America, according to him, to pass beyond vulgar, soulless democracy in the name of a new moral, affective, religious, and even metaphysical education of a nation capable of restoring Nature (the only complete poem) and of unifying the people under the idea of All. To democracy as a word with a rubbery nature and democracy as a banner, we could thus add democracy as an aesthetic program of spiritual renewal and as the promise of an egalitarian future (at least for some). The specificity of this figure of democracy is particularly palpable in the juxtaposition between Rimbaud's poem cited above entitled "Democracy," and one of the poems where Whitman summarizes his poetic orientation in *Leaves of Grass*:

FOR YOU, O DEMOCRACY
COME, I will make the continent indissoluble,
I will make the most splendid race the sun ever shone upon,
I will make the divine magnetic lands,
    With the love of comrades,
        With the life-long love of comrades.

I will plant companionship thick as trees along all the rivers of
    America, and along the shores of the great lakes, and all
    over the prairies,
I will make inseparable cities with their arms about each other's
    necks,
    By the love of comrades,
        By the manly love of comrades.

For you these from me, O Democracy, to serve you ma femme!
For you, for you I am trilling these songs.[82]

There was therefore never a simple historical shift by which the understanding of democracy definitively changed its meaning. Rather, it was a matter of a historical metastasis distributed in a specific manner through the three dimensions of history (and such a transformation is still ongoing). To take yet another example of a different sort, Karl Polanyi asserts that in the era of Chartism the liberals abhorred popular government and that "the concept of democracy was foreign to the English middle classes."[83] Even when the pro-democratic consensus began to impose itself, the notion of democracy remained a concept in struggle. In truth, it appears that the consensus was able to spread precisely due to the elasticity of the concept, and thus its use by antagonistic camps. It has brought together, among others, the liberal tradition and the Marxist tradition since approximately the middle of the nineteenth century.[84] Ferociously opposed at the ideological level, these two traditions make reference, minor exceptions aside, to the same political idea, and they thus illustrate perfectly well contemporary democratophilia. Of course, the liberals tend to identify democracy with the election of representatives and with a few conditions such as individual rights, whereas the socialists and communists contrast such a formal democracy with a substantive or real democracy, in which the people would be truly endowed with power. It was Lenin who summarized, in no uncertain terms, this antagonism: "In capitalist society we have a democracy that is curtailed, wretched, false, a democracy only for the rich, for the minority. The dictatorship of the proletariat, the period of transition to communism, will for the first time create democracy for the people, for the majority, along with the necessary suppression of the exploiters, of the minority. Communism alone is capable of providing really complete democracy."[85] In conformity with the Marxist thesis on the withering away of the state, he adds straightaway: "The more complete it is, the sooner it will become unnecessary and wither away of its own accord." This antagonism between two forms of democracy is obviously inscribed in a dialectic, and more precisely in what Herbert Marcuse called the "dialectics of democracy: if democracy means self-government of free people, with justice for all, then the realization of democracy would presuppose abolition of the existing pseudo-democracy."[86] Despite such differences, the democratic reference thus remains more or less a constant in liberalism, as in Marxism. And such a consensus continues today in a slightly different form insofar as numerous Marxists and Socialists have converted by becoming defenders of what is sometimes called radical democracy (if it is not simply liberal democracy). Proposing in diverse ways to break with the teleology of a certain form of traditional Marxism, they sometimes conceive of democracy as an interruption rather than as a state of affairs by way of a theoretical shift from being to event, from substance to act, from substantive to verb, from the state to political action, and more generally from a positive dialectic of synthesis to a negative dialectic of contradictions without end.

Among the at least partial exceptions, we could cite the "new reactionaries" (who at times lay claim to a form of liberalism) by referring in particular to the critical analysis proposed by Jacques Rancière in *Hatred of Democracy*. On the left, Alain Badiou has followed the path traced by Jean-Paul Sartre by flaunting a distrust of democracy, emphasizing the Marxist critique rather than its positive discourse on democracy. The author of the *Critique of Dialectical Reason* attacked universal human rights, representation, and democratic elections (see in particular *Anti-Semite and Jew* and essays such as "Are We in a Democracy?" and "Elections: A Trap for Fools"), which did not prevent him from making several laudatory references to democracy in very precise contexts.[87] Badiou has summarized his own stance as follows:

> Despite all that is devaluing the authority of the word *democracy* day after day, there is no doubt that this remains the dominant emblem of contemporary political society. An emblem is the "untouchable" in a symbolic system [ . . . ]. I therefore assert this: to simply touch upon the real of our societies, it's necessary, as an *a priori* exercise, to dislodge their emblem. We only make truth out of the world we're living in if we don't leave aside the word *democracy*, if we take the risk of not being a democrat, and thus of being heartily disapproved of by "everyone."[88]

Nevertheless, such stances remain very much the minority, and the libero-Marxian consensus on democracy constitutes merely one facet of an extremely widespread democratophilia. Without going into the details of its geographic and social distribution, which would take us too far afield, it behooves us to insist on its surprising ubiquity. From Wendy Brown to Robert Dahl, and including R. R. Palmer, Bertlinde Laniel, Pierre Rosanvallon, Raymond Williams, Sheldon Wolin, Eric Hobsawm, and many others, historians and theorists of democracy agree in saying that our conjuncture is absolutely unique insofar as this is the first time that there has existed a nearly unanimous approval of it:

> Today, the word "democracy/*démocratie*" everywhere evokes favorable feelings for the majority of people, and this is so often irrespective of the context in which it is used.[89]

Nobody now disputes that democracy is the most desirable type of political regime. This has not always been the case.[90]

The word "democracy" has today become a general symbol of widely held political and personal values.[91]

"Democracy" and "democratic" have become in the twentieth century words which imply approval of the society or institution so described.[92]

Democracy has historically unparalleled global popularity today [ ... ]. Democracy is exalted not only across the globe today but across the political spectrum. [ ... ] Berlusconi and Bush, Derrida and Balibar, Italian communists and Hamas—we are all democrats now.[93]

There are words [ ... ] for which everyone is anxious to demonstrate enthusiasm, such as mothers and the environment. Democracy is one of these. In the days of "really existing socialism," even the most implausible regimes laid claim to it in their official titles, as in North Korea, Pol Pot's Cambodia, and Yemen. Today, it is impossible, outside a few Islamic theocracies and Middle Eastern hereditary kingdoms and sheikhdoms, to find any regime that does not pay tribute to the idea of competitively elected assemblies or presidents.[94]

## Performative Contradictions of Actually Existing Democracy

Well, the first thing I want to say is: Mandate my ass! Because it seems as though we've been convinced that 26 percent of the registered voters, not even 26 percent of the American people, but 26 percent of the registered voters form a mandate or a landslide. 21 percent voted for Skippy and 3, 4 percent voted for somebody else who might have been running.
—Gil Scott-Heron on Ronald Reagan's election

There's no democratic state that's not compromised to the very core by its part in generating human misery.
—Gilles Deleuze

At the moment no one could be more for a democracy than I am. My objection is only that in no existing society, and surely not in those which call themselves democratic, does democracy exist. What exists is a kind of very

limited, illusory form of democracy that is beset with inequalities, while the true conditions of democracy have still to be created.
—Herbert Marcuse

By relying on an alternative logic of history, the above analysis does not aim at establishing the definitive version of the history of democracy but rather at altering the conceptual and perceptual apparatus in order to make other positivities emerge. In other words, a historical logic is not simply a different method for treating the same facts. It is a practical mode of intelligibility of history that furnishes givens that may be unthinkable or incomprehensible in other historical logics. For this reason, the references here and elsewhere to what could perhaps appear to some to be "empirical facts" are not to be taken as appeals to reality in the raw. It is a matter, instead, of evidential configurations, in a specific historical order, that attempt to make use of certain recognized truth practices in order to displace the logic of the predominant historical imaginary. Rather than a supposedly objective description of the real, this is an intervention aiming at reconfiguring the concept in struggle that is "reality."

The perspective shed above on the history of democracy should thus allow us to relativize its apparently incontestable value and help us to resist the normative blackmail of our conjuncture. The objective is to open a more focused inquiry into the illusory absolute political knowledge of our times. To do so, I will concentrate in what follows on an immanent notion of democracy that circulates in a very specific manner in our historical field in order to compare, in particular, the principles appealed to in its name with the practices that it appears to sanction. Obviously, it is not a matter of once again reifying democracy (or of falling into a blind positivism), but rather of analyzing it as a practical concept, a praxi-concept, with a certain consistency—which does not mean unicity—in the context where it takes root. I will therefore engage in a form of social epistemology that begins neither with the disincarnated unicity of concepts in themselves, nor with the radical heterogeneity of diverse definitions, but with a field of usages that evinces a certain internal consistency in a specific conjuncture of practices.

To this end, let us take the case of the ideological showcase of democracy that is the United States, even if the majority of our analysis will also apply mutatis mutandis to the other "Western democracies" and to numerous so-called international organizations. As is well known, the American government presents itself as the great bearer of the democratic torch. From the war to make the world "safe for democracy" (Woodrow Wilson) and the war to "save Europe" to the alleged attempt to export democracy to Iraq or elsewhere, few countries have laid claim with such vehemence to the absolute good that is the democratic cause.

We should understand the word *good* in the double meaning of the term, since it refers to a product as well as a value. If the United States presents itself as the defender of a value, it also purports to deliver a product. Just as with Coca-Cola and McDonald's, American-style democracy functions, at least in part, as a consumer good of the "free world." Yet, as we will see, the vigorous marketing of democracy is concerned more with the image of its product—with its label and logo—than with its content. Democracy has become, as Sheldon Wolin has clearly shown, "a brand name for a product manageable at home and marketable abroad."[95] He sketched the contours of what I propose to call the Janus face of contemporary democracy: it is at once the symbol of the political and social good par excellence and the vehicle of a pernicious project that it is perhaps necessary to describe, as we will see, as "anti-democratic."

With respect to the desire to see American-style democracy spread around the world, Noam Chomsky has asserted that "[no] belief concerning US foreign policy is more deeply entrenched."[96] Yet he immediately adds: "The faith in this doctrine may seem surprising. Even a cursory inspection of the historical record reveals that a persistent theme in American foreign policy has been the subversion and overthrow of parliamentary regimes, and the resort to violence to destroy popular organizations that might offer the majority of the population an opportunity to enter the political arena."[97] This does not mean that U.S. foreign policy is systematically opposed to democracy. With few exceptions, the American government has generally supported or at least tolerated, in its own way, pro-business Western democracies. The ever-important question of public relations is at stake and, as we shall see, democracy can be absolutely acceptable as long as it remains truly an American-style democracy, which is to say "a political system with regular elections but no serious challenge to business rule."[98]

We will return later to the specificity of the domestic policy of American-style democracy. For now, let us briefly review its foreign affairs. William

Blum, the former State Department employee who became one of its most severe and encyclopedic critics, drew up a disturbing balance sheet of American interventions since the end of the Second World War, and there are numerous cases of overturning democratically elected governments. He also emphasized Washington's meddling in elections, as it has not hesitated to invest considerable sums and to use very dubious tactics—from misinformation campaigns and economic destabilization efforts to clandestine CIA operations—to swing so-called democratic elections in a direction favorable to its own interests. In one of his most recent books, entitled quite simply *America's Deadliest Export: Democracy*, he reaches the conclusion that the American administration, for which the question of democracy remains utterly secondary, aims above all at world domination. For the United States has shown itself to be hostile to any popular movement likely to contest its hegemony. It is in this vein that it has

- endeavored to overthrow more than 50 foreign governments, most of which were democratically elected;
- grossly interfered in democratic elections in at least 30 countries;
- attempted to assassinate more than 50 foreign leaders;
- dropped bombs on the people of more than 30 countries;
- attempted to suppress a populist or nationalist movement in 20 countries.[99]

Needless to say, such a performance inevitably calls into question the history of the spectacular blossoming of democracy. Numerous other specialists have corroborated Blum's conclusions, often with detailed investigations bearing on individual cases of what Chomsky judiciously named "deterring democracy."[100]

These are the kinds of abuses that had incited Martin Luther King Jr. to forcefully declare in 1963: "I knew that I could never again raise my voice against the violence of the oppressed in the ghettos without having first spoken clearly to the greatest purveyor of violence in the world today—my own government."[101] These activities obviously continue unabated in the contemporary conjuncture.[102] In addition to military and paramilitary interventions, as well as the growing and dangerous use of armed mercenaries,[103] we should recall a series of recent developments, on which it would be extremely difficult to affix the label, or rather the fig leaf, of "democracy." Take, for instance, the revelations concerning the existence of a global network of secret CIA prisons, or again the numerous international prisons known for their deplorable reputation, including those of Guantánamo and Abu Ghraib, not to mention the fact that the United States has by far the highest per capita incarceration rate as well as the largest prison population in the world (without even mentioning, as well, the racial demographics, the existence of the death penalty, or the mistreatment of detainees).[104] The incarceration of more than 2 million people on American soil, of which the majority are persons of color often having lost the right to vote and other rights (as well as future prospects), drove Michelle Alexander to draw the conclusion that there exists a caste system and that "America is still not an egalitarian democracy."[105] Let us also make note of the program known under the incredible euphemism "extraordinary rendition," by which the American government takes the liberty of kidnapping, transferring, detaining, and torturing (or having tortured) any suspect, no matter where in the world, independently of national and international laws. The sordid redefinition of torture by the Office of Legal Counsel likewise deserves to be highlighted, since it is capable of preventing legal proceedings against those responsible for torture (in the everyday sense of the term).[106] Let us also not forget the USA PATRIOT Act; the Military Commissions Act; the staggering proliferation of illegal wiretapping; the systematic collection of metadata by the NSA and more generally its utterly unbridled espionage; the orchestrated attack on whistle-blowers such as Chelsea Manning, Julian Assange, and Edward Snowden; or, again, the famous "kill list" allowing the American president to have any suspect killed, anywhere in the world, without legal proceedings and without due process.[107]

A large part of the world population is perfectly aware of these activities, of which they often have more or less direct experience. It is precisely for this reason that it would perhaps not be absurd to allow all citizens or persons of the world—or, at least, those whose fate is largely determined by the actions of the U.S. government—to vote in American elections. If the life of a people depends directly on the decisions of a set of political representatives, should they not have their say in a democracy? In the end, and despite the fact that its foreign affairs attest much too often to practices that numerous people would judge to be anti-democratic, is not the United States a democratic country?

It is this crucial question that I would now like to address by concentrating on two parallel definitions of the so-called power of the people in the contemporary world: the legal definition of democracy as a political regime founded on the declaration of fundamental rights, and its procedural definition as a political system regularly having recourse to free elections.[108] It is true that the American republic ratified ten amendments to its constitution in 1791, which aim at guaranteeing a certain number of rights for its citizens, including freedom of religion, freedom of expression, freedom of the press, the right to assemble, and habeas corpus. This Bill of Rights, which is inscribed in the tradition of political liberalism, remains a major reference point for the protection of citizens against the abuses of the state. It has played a very important role in numerous sociopolitical struggles that one could qualify as democratic. One must not forget, however, that it was written in an age when an overwhelming majority of the population of America did not benefit from all the rights of citizenship, whether it be the indigenous population, slaves, or women. Although it freely uses a universalist discourse, like numerous other documents by the so-called Founding Fathers, it was obvious at the time that certain persons simply were not members of the people.[109] To enjoy these rights, it was first necessary to be recognized as having a right to them; yet there was never a universal declaration of the right to rights. The Bill of Rights thereby manifests a dangerous discursive hegemony by which a particular group, which was in fact a minority (as a general rule, property-owning males who were believers and of European descent),[110] endeavored to pass itself off as the universal by pretending to be the people as a whole. What is called *equality before the law* presupposes *inequality before the law*. This is the paradox of political equality under liberalism: it presupposes a more fundamental inequality as its sine qua non condition.

Let us not be duped, in this respect, by Whig historiography, which emphasizes all of the historical progress that has allowed the indigenous, African Americans, women, and others to be recognized—up to a certain point—as citizens. For this primordial inequality still exists today and continues to haunt political liberalism. This is not only due to the persistent oppression of the indigenous population, to racism, and to the patriarchy, as well as economic oppression, xenophobia, ableism, heteronormativity, and gender and sexual normativity. It is also the case that certain social categories, the precise delimitation of which remains malleable, quite simply do not have the right to the same rights, whether it be the insane, the cognitively challenged, the depraved, criminals, detainees, minors, "immigrants," or foreigners. In the form of political liberalism at work in the American system, we could thus say that we "all" have the same rights, except for all of those who do not have the right to them, and who therefore are not part of the "we." The right to rights constitutes a fundamental question that touches on the meta-legal delimitation of the domain of the law and, as a consequence, on a certain form of democracy in the contemporary world.

In addition to these structural inequalities, there likewise exist what one could call circumstantial inequalities, to the extent that the American state has not held back, on numerous occasions, from crossing the boundaries established by the Bill of Rights, often by means of a redefinition of those having the right to rights. Somewhat ironically, the justification of such acts frequently takes the form of an appeal to the protection of rights: in order to guarantee *our* most inalienable rights, we must take them away from others. Put differently, in order to assure our rights, it is necessary that certain persons not have the right to them. If we concentrate solely on the present situation—leaving aside major historical cases such as that of the internment during the Second World War of some 120,000 individuals of Japanese descent, two-thirds of whom were American citizens—we can cite the USA PATRIOT Act, which allows for the limitless detention of American citizens with neither warrant nor indictment, without a trial, without legal representation, and without even the possibility of contacting one's family. As Michael Parenti has noted, all of this is "in violation of the fifth, sixth, and fourteenth amendments."[111] After the Edward Snowden revelations concerning the extremely widespread spying by the NSA, which flouts the Fourth Amendment, the former American president Jimmy Carter firmly asserted: "America does not have a functioning democracy at this point in time."[112] The fact that the FISA court, which is actually supposed to oversee the activities of the NSA, meets clandestinely led Glenn Greenwald, a constitutional lawyer and one of the journalists who worked with Snowden on his revelations, to write: "How can you have a democracy in which your rights are determined in total secrecy by a secret court issuing 80-page rulings about what rights you have as a citizen? It is Orwellian and absurd."[113] It is all the more aberrant that it has been shown that the surveillance network has in no way helped find so-called terrorists. Of the 225 cases of terrorism since September 11, 2001, studied by the New American Foundation, the American metadata collected by the NSA has played an initiating role in the discovery of conspiracies in just one single case: that of four individuals who apparently sent $8,500 to a militant group in Somalia.[114] We could also cite the recent infringements on the freedom of assembly during the violent repression of the Occupy movement, while bearing in mind that the criminalization of dissent haunts the entire history of the United States. For among the protesters who exercised, as I did, their supposed constitutional right "peaceably to assemble" (First Amendment), 7,775 were arrested in 122 different cities and hundreds were injured by the police in the forceful interventions orchestrated by the Department of Homeland Security.[115] In truth, one might have the impression that we all have inalienable rights in this democracy, as long as we do not actually exercise them.

It is obviously not a question here of indiscriminately lumping things together by suggesting, for instance, that American democracy is in the process of committing the same atrocities as various totalitarian regimes. Each political configuration has its own proper consistency, and it is necessary to take stock of this. It is useful to mention, in this respect, Sheldon Wolin's insightful analysis in *Democracy Incorporated*. He is interested, in this work, in what he proposes to call inverted totalitarianism, which is to say "a new type of political system, seemingly one driven by abstract totalizing powers, not by personal rule, one that succeeds by encouraging political disengagement rather than mass mobilization, that relies more on 'private' media than on public agencies to disseminate propaganda reinforcing the official version of events."[116] On all of these fronts, inverted totalitarianism distinguishes itself very precisely from traditional totalitarianism, and Wolin rightly insists on such differences. One of the fundamental aspects of inverted totalitarianism is what he calls "antidemocracy." This is not an overt attack on the very idea of popular government but is rather a civic demobilization that is promoted at all levels: "Citizens are encouraged to distrust their government and politicians; to concentrate upon their own interests; to begrudge their taxes; and to exchange active involvement for symbolic gratifications of patriotism, collective self-righteousness, and military prowess."[117] He thus draws a parallel between the "strong" democracy of the United States and inverted totalitarianism, on the one hand, and weak democracy and classic totalitarianism, on the other: "Our thesis, however, is this: it is possible for a form of totalitarianism, different from the classical one, to evolve from a putatively 'strong democracy' instead of a 'failed' one. A weak democracy that fails, such as that of Weimar, might end in classical totalitarianism, while a failed strong democracy might lead to inverted totalitarianism."[118]

The expression *strong democracy* could obviously lead to confusion. For in the United States, and more generally in the contemporary world, the most appropriate term would perhaps be *oligarchy*.[119] It is not simply a matter, as is often said, of a representative democracy where a small group of politicians apparently undertake to represent the interests of the people. If one holds absolutely to the term *democracy*, it must be noted that this is effectively an un-representative democracy. The interests of the people and the common good remain entirely secondary to other interests, notably those of the *oligos*. Cornelius Castoriadis perfectly describes this situation: "I have always thought," he writes,

> that so-called representative democracy is not a true democracy. Its representatives only minimally represent the people who elect them. First they represent themselves or represent particular interests, the lobbies, etc. And, even if that wasn't the case, to say that someone is going to represent me in an irrevocable manner for 5 years amounts to saying that I divest myself of my sovereignty as part of the people. Rousseau already said this: the English believe that they are free because they elect representatives every 5 years, but they are free only one day every 5 years: the day of the election.[120]

It should be specified, for methodological reasons, that the judgments put forth here do not aim in the least at attaching a specific concept to an era while purporting to identify its proper nature once and for all. It is instead a matter of intervening in contemporary discourse by sketching a topological capture of the current conjuncture, which means to make a proposition—starting from a specific perspective in the sociohistorical world—in order to grasp, heuristically, the basic outline of a certain field of forces. Rather than a supposedly objective description of the real, it is thus a question of a circumspect intervention into a reality in struggle.

This un-representative oligarchy is, more precisely still, a plutocratic oligarchy: it is the few, with extraordinary means, who govern the many.

To speak simply of a minority nevertheless runs the risk, however, of missing the point, since the *oligos*, in its contemporary form, constitutes in truth an infinitesimal percentage of the population. This minuscule fringe of the minority, which it would be appropriate to call the plutocratic aristocracy, desperately tries, of course, to legitimize its reign through the administration of a representative democracy (without veritable representation). Yet this does not change anything regarding the real distribution of power. *The government of the people* means the management and control of the *dēmos*, and not at all the government by and for the *dēmos*. Wolin himself openly recognizes that we are not in a democracy and that the very term is hardly suitable in the case of the United States: "If we were to list the essentials of a democracy, such as rule by the people, we would find that democracy in that sense is nonexistent—and that may be a substantial part of the crisis that is no crisis."[121] Kristin Ross comes to a very similar conclusion: "Democracy had become a class ideology justifying systems that allowed a very small number of people to govern—and to govern without the people, so to speak; systems that seem to exclude any other possibility than the infinite reproduction of their own functioning."[122] The wolf of oligarchy seems in fact to have procured a sheepskin in order to better mix in with the flock of lambs. Yet if one looks closely and from a different angle, one cannot but catch sight of it. Whence comes the necessity of prohibiting in advance any deep investigation and any change in perspective by accusing those who pose challenging questions of being anti-democratic and anti-patriotic, of not respecting the values of the flock, of being paranoid, of wanting to create problems where there are none. Hands off the democratic sheepskin!

The oligarchic principle according to which the small number governs the larger number is found not only in the governmental structure, but also in political power and in the institutions of the state, not to mention in economic structures. With respect to elections, for instance, it is necessary to recall that it is not the people who vote, but citizens having the right to vote, and more precisely those who see a reason to do so and take the necessary steps to overcome the obstacles erected by the political system in order to register to vote. If one adds up all of those who are deprived of the right to vote (minors, prisoners, certain ex-convicts, foreigners, the insane, the mentally challenged, women until relatively recently, and other "incompetents"), those who see no reason to vote (abstention wins a prodigious number of democratic elections, perhaps even the majority), and those who have seen their access to ballot boxes limited by restrictive measures, there can be a very significant percentage of the population—at times a majority, as with every presidential election in America since at least World War II[123]—that does not participate in the electoral process. This varies considerably, of course, depending on the country, and it is very important to examine the analytic and evaluative criteria used to judge democratic processes, which have a tendency to grant a considerable privilege to democracies deemed Western.[124] Jimmy Carter's position is interesting in this respect, since it goes against the image of democracy in the American mass media. He defended Venezuela as having one of the best electoral procedures in the world, while juxtaposing it to that of the United States, which he did not hesitate to identify as being among the worst.[125] Since this is not the place to consider all of the details, let us restrict ourselves to emphasizing a characteristic feature of our primary example: "The United States ranks among the lowest in the world in voter turnout. Nearly a third of adult Americans are not even registered to vote."[126]

Furthermore, it is not the people or the citizens who decide on what to vote, on which political program, at what time, and so on. It is the oligarchs and the oligarchic system that decide on this and that submit their choice to the vote of the electorate (in certain very specific cases). One could legitimately wonder, for instance, why there are not more referendums, and in particular referendums of popular initiative, in "democracy." Cornelius Castoriadis perfectly described this state of affairs when he wrote: "The election is rigged, not because the ballot boxes are being stuffed, but because the options are determined in advance. They are told, 'vote for or against the Maastricht Treaty,' for example. But who made the Maastricht Treaty? It isn't us."[127] It would thus be naive to believe that elections reflect public opinion or even the preferences of the electorate. For these oligarchic principles dominate our societies to such an extent that the nature of the choice is decided in advance. In the case of elections, it is the powerful media apparatus—financed in the United States by private interests, big business, and the bureaucratic machinery of party politics—that presents to the electorate the choices to be made, the viable candidates, the major themes to be debated, the range of possible positions, the questions to be raised and pondered, the statistical tendencies of "public opinion," the viewpoint of experts, and the positions taken by the most prominent politicians.[128] What we call political debate and public space (which is properly speaking a space of publicity) are formatted to such an extent that we are encouraged to make binary choices without ever asking ourselves genuine questions: we must be either for or against a particular political star, a specific publicity campaign, such or such "societal problem." "One of the many reasons why it is laughable to speak of 'democracy' in Western societies today," asserts Castoriadis, "is because the 'public' sphere is in fact private—be it in France, the United States, or England."[129] The market of ideas is saturated, and the political consumer is asked to passively choose a product that is already on the shelves. This is despite the fact that the contents of the products are often more or less identical, conjuring up in many ways the difference that exists between a brand-name product on the right, with the shiny packaging of the tried-and-true, and a generic product on the left, that aspires to be more amenable to the people. "Free elections do not necessarily express 'the will of the people,'" Erich Fromm judiciously wrote. "If a highly advertised brand of toothpaste is used by the majority of the people because of some fantastic claims it makes in its propaganda, nobody with any sense would say that people have 'made a decision' in favor of the toothpaste. All that could be claimed is that the propaganda was sufficiently effective to coax millions of people into believing its claims."[130]

It is of the utmost importance, in this respect, to note that the U.S. Supreme Court decided in 2010—in the name, moreover, of a stupendous interpretation of the constitutional principle of the freedom of expression—to not prevent the financial contribution of businesses, associations, and trade unions to electoral campaigns. The freedom of expression, which is supposed to guarantee in some sense the freedom of thought (*pensée*), has become—and this is not entirely new—the freedom to spend, and thus to un-think (*dé-penser*). If so-called democratic elections were already oligarchic publicity campaigns, they are increasingly being transformed into auctions where the candidates of the economic oligarchy are bought, body and soul, before being given a makeover and resold to the public in exorbitantly expensive spectacles.[131] The Citizens United decision was only one step in a long process of financializing the political world, which dates back some time and which continues to gain ground today with *McCutcheon v. FEC*. This decision in 2014 by the

American Supreme Court abolishes, once again in the name of the freedom of expression, the limits fixed for financial contributions in federal elections. In such a context, it is not at all surprising that the majority of the alleged representatives of the people are today millionaires.[132] The neologism that Robert McChesney and Michael Nichols have proposed for describing such a system—*dollarocracy*—is thus appropriate at several levels: "We have a system that is now defined more by one dollar, one vote than by one person, one vote. We live in a society where a small number of fabulously wealthy individuals and giant corporations control most of the dollars—and by extension have most of the political power."[133] In a recent study, Martin Gilens and Benjamin I. Page have shown through a multivariable statistical analysis that, in effect, "economic elites and organized groups representing business interests have substantial independent impacts on U.S. government policy, while average citizens and mass-based interest groups have little or no independent influence."[134]

The case of WikiLeaks provides a particularly revealing illustration of the relationship between so-called freedom of expression and the power of the status quo. Although the Obama administration, and specifically Hillary Clinton, ran out of breath declaring, particularly against China, that the circulation of information is a fundamental principle of the freedom of expression and thus of democracy, it engaged in a ferocious attack—with the complete support of the business world and a significant portion of the press—against WikiLeaks and against the circulation of information directly calling into question the American government.[135] Is it necessary to draw the conclusion that we are effectively free to say all of the banalities we wish (as is too often the case on television shows and in the press), as long as we never truly call into question the systems in place, as long as we never express genuine criticisms? Is the freedom of expression, under contemporary oligarchies, not at base a simple *freedom of verbiage* whereby we are free to say anything *so long as it is meaningless*, that is, so long as it remains an innocuous expression that never challenges the status quo? Truly free expression, which sometimes expresses what does not want to be heard: does it not awaken, almost inevitably, the *freedom of repression* of so-called democratic governments? Isn't this the primary freedom guaranteed in democracy?

To return to elections, it should be noted that the lack of proportional representation favors the artificial inflation of the power of the established political parties and the marginalization of alternative parties. This explains in part why "voter turnout ranges from 36 to 42 percent for congressional elections, while in countries that have PR [proportional representation], turnouts range from 70 to 90 percent."[136] In addition, we should highlight the systematic attack on the exercise of the right to vote (which is not guaranteed by the U.S. Constitution),[137] whether it consists in gerrymandering, in excessive restrictions on voter registration, in the use of electronic voting machines managed by private corporations, or in other strategies that make the act of voting difficult or pointless for the people.[138]

It is therefore hardly surprising that, according to public opinion polls, American citizens do not feel represented by their government. "In a New York Times/CBS poll," writes Michael Parenti, "79 percent of respondents agreed that government is 'pretty much run by a few big interests looking out for themselves.'"[139] According to the Rasmussen Reports, only 35 percent of the American population finds elections to be fair, and only one person in ten thinks that the members of Congress get reelected due to the quality of their work.[140] Moreover, nearly half of the population believes that the two political parties do not represent the American people and that Congress is corrupt.[141] Based on a recent study by the Pew Research Center, not more than approximately three Americans in ten, during the last seven years, "have said they trust the federal government to do the right thing always or most of the time."[142] A majority of Americans say, as well, according to the same study, that "the federal government is a threat to their personal rights and freedoms."

These polls provide, in the end, a remarkable portrait of what "the people" think of "their" government. It is thus clear that the American public is not completely duped, and that there exists a highly significant discrepancy between the people and power in what is called a regime founded on the power of the people. Without diminishing the importance of such a discrepancy, which precisely illustrates the sociogeographic variability of the encroachment of oligarchic principles, it is important not to fall into the trap of a schematic opposition between the pure conscience of the citizen or individual and the powerful political machinery that imposes itself from on high. A political order, as I propose to understand it here, is not simply a set of governmental institutions and actions. It is more profoundly a system of values, perceptions, thoughts, affects, and activities that has been collectively forged (which does not necessarily presuppose the equality of the actors involved). I am obviously not seeking to define, here or elsewhere, the true nature or the essence of politics. It is rather a question of proposing an interventionist concept of politics, which is to say a conceptualization forged in a specific conjuncture that aims at reconfiguring a given field of conceptuality by elaborating another way of understanding what "political" means or could mean. According to this conception, there is no pure citizen or immaculate individual. There are produced and self-producing political subjects in a theoretico-practical matrix that forms them and that they form. By saying that we are not currently in a democracy, I also mean that in contemporary society there hardly exists any "democratic" training, in the sense of a collective and generalized political education of the citizens. Castoriadis put his finger on this fundamental problem by insisting on the need to reinvent *paideia*: "So democracy—this is what's important—is a matter of educating citizens, something that does not at all exist today."[143] In describing the contemporary situation, he makes reference to a veritable counter-education of the people: "All political life aims precisely at making them forget how to govern. It aims at convincing them that there are experts to whom matters must be entrusted. There is thus a political counter-education. Whereas people should accustom themselves to exercising all sorts of responsibilities and taking initiatives, they accustom themselves to following the options that others present to them or voting for those options. And since people are far from being stupid, the result is that they believe in it less and less, and they become cynical, in a kind of political apathy."[144] The societies we live in are thus largely oligarchic in the way in which they produce and form subjects. Whether it be in the educational system, in other public or private institutions, or in the media, oligarchy tends to regulate and manage our political socialization.

From this comes the need for a political anthropology as the basis for a new social pedagogy. For in a situation like this, it is insufficient to proclaim democratic principles like free elections and the principle of the majority (or to fall back into the Whig history of political liberalism by professing that we shall all *one day* have the same rights). If there is no collective political *Bildung*, such principles can quite simply serve to consolidate the reigning oligarchy, which is partially founded on the destitution of collective education, not to mention extremely vast and powerful disinformation campaigns. "A numerical majority," Daniel Bensaïd aptly explained, "is never proof of truth or justice."[145] What is called *politics* does not begin with the act of voting or even with becoming committed. Before going to the ballot box or arriving at the supposed age of political maturity, we are already formed by a system of values, a framework of understanding, a complex of desires, a conception of history, a certain vision of the world, in brief, an entire political imaginary. In a universe largely dominated by the rampant morality of each for him- or herself, large-scale counter-education, the fabrication of legitimate needs and desires, a triumphalist historical logic, and a Manichean vision of a world torn between the alleged forces of good (meaning "democratic") and the supposed forces of evil ("terrorist" or "tyrannical"), it is necessary to return to the crucial question of the social formation of political agents, without settling for an analysis of governmental institutions or political actions in the traditional sense of the term. "We would have to seek," Wendy Brown rightly states, "knowledge and control of the multiple forces that construct us as subjects, produce the norms through which we conceive reality and deliberate about the good, and present the choices we face when voting or even legislating."[146] This would allow us to circumvent the moralizing controversies that gravitate around value-concepts such as democracy in favor of a more fundamental investigation into the type of political and economic society we should construct and the forms of subjectivity we want to favor. Exhausted by struggles, spread thin by conflicts, deprived of meaning so as to be better invested with connotations, the term *democracy* deserves perhaps to be put out to pasture, even if only provisionally. This would be done in the name of a broader political struggle, which could potentially appeal to other practical philosophemes and other interventionist concepts, such as *revolution* and *isonomy*, which have, for that matter, the advantage of referring to the most fundamental structures of a sociopolitical order. The notion of isonomia is interesting in this regard, since its etymological origin is not linked to command/government/foundation (*archē*) or to power (*kratos*), as is obviously the case for the three forms of government identified since Antiquity (monarchy, oligarchy, democracy). It would perhaps be possible—but this is not the place for such an undertaking—to distinguish in this way between forms of government and political orders in the broad sense of the term. Indeed, the suffix *-nomos* and the idea of an "equality before the law/norm" seem to indicate a field that is vaster than that of the government.

Here we touch on the very core of politics. It is important to resist its reduction to government, meaning to an authority or to a set of institutions that are supposed to manage society. Whereas the government corresponds to a political regime of the state, what I propose to call *politics*—heuristically and in order to intervene into a specific conceptual field—is nothing less than the collective construction of the collectivity. It is a common project of forging norms, values, *Weltanschauungen*, desires, practices, bodies, actions, and institutions, in short, of forming the *res publicae* in all of their diverse aspects. Politics is not limited, therefore, to governmental organizations and their activities. It is, more broadly, the practice that consists in constructing a common world, a *cosmos*. Any discussion of democracy in the governmental sense of the term that ignores politics quite simply neglects the ecosystem that produces and gives meaning—and direction—to government.

What Is the Use of the Purification of the Political?

Is a democracy, such as we know it, the last improvement possible in government?
—Henry David Thoreau

The magnetism of the democratic idea is such that its setbacks and failures, even profound ones, are not necessarily capable of calling it into question.[147] The Idea remains pure, and this purity is the bearer of a promise: democracy, if it is not yet perfect, remains to come. It will perhaps always remain to come.[148] What does it matter, then, if the valorization of this idea is recent, or if actual practices are not worthy of the name? Would not all of this highlight even more the eminence of the democratic Idea and the significance of its historical recognition by "us"?

If the purity of the political idea lies downstream from current practices, the tabula rasa is upstream. These are two neighboring notions that complement each other insofar as they are both founded on the idea of an independent political sphere. The common root of the purity of the political idea and of the tabula rasa, which presupposes the existence of an original scene on which the political would come to institute itself as a distinct domain, is thus what I propose to call quite simply *the purity of the political*.

The question of the best form of government is naturally inscribed in this framework. If the institution of a political order began at zero, in the sense that it was a matter of establishing, most often independently of the sociohistorical and cultural conjuncture, an order that functions more or less autonomously, then it would perhaps make sense to search for the optimal plan for the institution of the political sphere. Obviously, this is not to say that there actually exists a tabula rasa in the sense of an absolutely pure and distinct foundation. Each point of departure has its own qualities, but it is usually formally unique, homogeneous, and general, even if it is for one specific "culture" or "civilization." In the constitution of the political order, whatever its range may be, there is *a* square one, whether it be a state of the world, an alleged historical moment of humanity, character traits of supposed human nature, a hypothetical original position, or any other common starting point for the analysis of the best form of government *in general*.

The same appears to be true, with one important difference, for culturalist approaches that defend the position according to which square one would be a cultural stage, which is to say a supposed level of civilization. Although the universal dimension is partially called into question (unless one supposes that all societies are able to attain this at a given moment), the idea of a tabula rasa in the sense of a general starting point for the question of the best form of government remains. However, it becomes cultural or civilizational. This is the source of the very problematic conclusion that democracy is the best form of government for "all civilized societies," but also that there still exist cultures bogged down in forms of barbarism of such a sort that they have not yet attained the necessary level of civilization—which is understood to be the starting point for a veritable government—in order to establish a true political order.

Yet if the intransitive history of democracy and the contemporary contradictions of actually existing democracy have revealed anything, it is precisely that a *terra nullius* has never existed in politics. There has never been a virginal state of nature, a Garden of Eden, a general state of the world, a human nature, a homogeneous point of departure, or an absolute beginning. Politics has always already begun in the middle, interlaced with a long history of cultural practices (to such an extent that it lacks transhistorical and extrasocial conceptual unity). We cannot magically extract ourselves from it by restarting from scratch, despite what the faith in the purity of the political would lead us to think. It follows from this that there is no best form of government in general, nor a perfect plan, nor an ideal political system. This does not mean that there cannot be political projects or objectives, or that it would not be useful sometimes to speak of politics heuristically in order to indicate something distinct or something that should be distinguished in certain cases. It is even less a question of preventing any investigation into the concrete modi operandi of so-called systems of government, which requires, in fact, accounting for all the material institutions and practices that give them meaning.

If there is no tabula rasa in politics, this is not only for historical and cultural reasons; it is also for social reasons. There is no impermeable barrier between the political and other sociocultural practices. A "democracy" under the reign of neoliberal capitalism is something very different from the practices deemed democratic in prefeudal societies, among Amerindians, or in socialism, communism, or anarchism. It would even be necessary to inquire into whether or not a single and unique concept would truly be suitable for all of these practices, which are sometimes incompatible. Indeed, one cannot neatly separate the political from the economic, the cultural, or, in short, from an entire social world. What, in effect, would the political be if it were not profoundly rooted in the cultural practices and institutions of a socioeconomic universe?

As Angela Davis has reminded us so poignantly in her discussion of democracy under capitalism: "We know that there is a glaring incongruity between democracy and the capitalist economy which is the source of our ills. Regardless of all rhetoric to the contrary, the people are not the ultimate matrix of the laws and the system which govern them—certainly not black people and other nationally oppressed people, but not even the mass of whites. The people do not exercise decisive control over the determining factors of their lives."[149] There is reason to question, moreover, whether capitalist democracy favors or fuels highly reprehensible political activities, if it be colonialism and neocolonialism, the rise to power of certain forms of fascism, racial segregation and sexist discrimination (de jure or de facto), the upsurge of what Wolin calls inverted totalitarianism, or the rise of political schemers like George W. Bush and Silvio Berlusconi. It must be noted that the history of institutionalized democracy, as we know it, instead of being the history of a simple ascension toward the summum bonum of politics in general, is in fact punctuated by such practices.

The purification of the political can easily transform democracy into a fig leaf, notably by obfuscating or masking the diverse forms of injustice at work in a society whose government is judged to be democratic. By acting as if it were possible to neatly separate the form of government from economic, military, cultural, racial, sexual, or other modes of oppression, governmental responsibility is often removed (in the eyes of some). The case of Colombia is relatively revealing in this respect. It presents itself under the democratic label, and it has in effect seen a succession, practically uninterrupted, of governments based on so-called democratic representation. Yet as Eric Hobsbawm explained so well: "Although the country has not been involved in international wars, the number of people killed, maimed and driven from their homes in Colombia over the past half-century runs into millions. Almost certainly it far exceeds that in any other country of the western hemisphere. It is certainly larger than in any of the countries of that continent notoriously plagued with military dictatorships."[150] According to the logic of the purification of the political, such activities do not call into question what truly matters: at least it is a democracy! It is certainly appropriate to recall that the National Socialist Party was also democratically elected in Germany by winning the legislative elections in 1932 and that the head of the party, Adolf Hitler, was named chancellor by the president in 1933, in conformity with the rules of democracy. If there is a tendency to forget this, it is in part because the term *democracy* has been invested with moralizing forces to such an extent that it has lost its ability to discriminate. A dividing line has indeed been dug between, on the one hand, the factual democracies according to their institutional framework that nevertheless are not deserving of the name—we can think, for example, of Palestine and the elections won by Hamas, or of the Venezuela of the Bolivarian revolution—and, on the other hand, the states worthy of the name independently of the existence or nonexistence of veritably democratic institutions and practices. To deserve the name, it is not necessary to be democratic. Proof of this is to be found in all of the countries deemed democratic that are clearly less so than those that are not worthy of the name, including countries overtly hostile to any semblance of democracy, which nevertheless don the cherished logo of the contemporary world. Ultimately, it appears that democracy in name is so much more important than democracy in act.

The dangers of the purification of the political surpass the absolution of governments judged to be worthy of the worthiest name in politics. Indeed, the separation of the government from its political inscription, in the broad sense of the term, often goes hand in hand with the rarefaction of political acts. From the point of view of "democratic" citizens, for instance, the political is defined in extremely exceptional terms. Rousseau already highlighted this in a different context, by recalling that the English people are not "free" except at the very moment of elections (when they actually lose their freedom). But it is William Blum who draws the ultimate consequences from this for the contemporary world in a trenchant criticism of "60-second democracy," or what others have called "low-intensity democracy."[151] His critique should be cited in extenso, without losing sight of other ways of purging the political by limiting it to extremely circumscribed acts:[152]

> A nation with hordes of hungry, homeless, unattended sick, barely literate, unemployed and/or tortured people, whose loved ones are being disappeared and/or murdered with state connivance, can be said to be living in a "democracy"—its literal Greek meaning of "rule of the people" implying that this is the kind of life the people actually want—provided that every two years or four years they have the right to go to a designated place and put an X next to the name of one or another individual who promises to relieve their miserable condition, but who will, typically, do virtually nothing of the kind; and provided further that in this society there is at least a certain minimum of freedom—how much being in large measure a function of one's wealth—for one to express one's views about the powers-that-be and the workings of society, without undue fear of punishment, regardless of whether expressing these views has any influence whatsoever over the way things are.[153]

It is thus not simply that the purity of the political is a myth. It is that the purification of the political is usually part of a detrimental political project. Separating the governmental system from its socioeconomic inscription is equivalent to sterilizing the political by excluding social and cultural life from the political domain. One thus acts as if it were quite simply necessary to establish the best form of government—often by a *Blitzkrieg* bringing about quick elections[154]—without being concerned with politics in the broad sense of the term, meaning the collective fabrication of a shared cosmos.

If one were absolutely dedicated to recuperating the term and the practice of democracy, which obviously is not my argument here, it would be necessary to recognize that democratic rights remain purely formal and valueless as long as the material conditions of their actualization are lacking. Numerous have been those who have rightly reminded us that democratic government does not deserve its name as long as there is not a minimum of socioeconomic equality. This was one of the arguments of the citizens of Pennsylvania who fought against economic inequality in the 1780s. The politician William Findley perfectly summarized their concerns in asserting that the "biggest threat to democracy [ . . . ] was the growing gap between the rich and everyone else."[155] One finds a very similar idea in the county of Mecklenburg, North Carolina, when the delegates chosen in 1776 received instructions to draft a state constitution that promotes a "simple democracy, or as near as possible" by opposing the concentration of power in the hands of the rich.[156] Echoes are also found in France, for example in Babeuf's and Robespierre's opposition to censual suffrage and to the creation of a new economico-political aristocracy. "As soon as the property owned by citizens is the measure of their political rights," wrote Babeuf, "these rights must abide by the proportion of the properties owned."[157] As for Robespierre, it is interesting to note, beyond his rejection of censual suffrage, that his project of a Declaration of the Rights of Man and of the Citizen explicitly limited property: "The right to property is limited, like all others, by the obligation to respect the rights of others."[158] Even if they did not attain all of their objectives, the idea continued to make its way. One finds it today in the writings of authors such as Michael Parenti: "The contradictory nature of 'capitalist democracy' is that it professes egalitarian political principles while generating enormous disparities in material well-being and political influence."[159] He contrasts this to an economico-political definition of democracy that directly opposes the purification of the political: "Whether a political system is democratic or not depends not only on its procedures but on the actual material benefits and the social justice or injustice it propagates."[160] Thus, instead of blindly trusting in the received idea according to which democracy is quite simply the best form of government (particularly when it is purged of all of its impurities), it is important to ask ourselves whether *this* actually existing democracy—which, for instance, justifies neocolonial imperialism abroad and vigorously opposes the real, informed participation of citizens—is really and truly the best form of governance.

The study of actually existing democracy is indeed of the greatest importance for those who would like to rehabilitate the notion and the practice of democracy. For the time being, I have chosen another tactic, which consists in opening a breach in the current consensus in order to clear a space for reflection and action that is not already immediately colonized by the prevailing political imaginary. By refusing to submit straightaway to the exigencies of "our age," and by resisting the compulsion to stake out conformist positions, it is not only a matter of recognizing that every era is constructed by a complex field of forces (with significant political stakes), producing preordained paths of thought. It is also a question of creating an alternative historical order allowing us to approach, in an entirely different manner, the question of the development of politics "itself" and that of the contemporary conjuncture. This is in order to entirely rethink some of the major presuppositions of political theory and of the conceptualization of democracy today. Obviously, this does not mean that we must maintain at all costs a purely critical stance, but it has been necessary here to swim against the current.[161]

In order to resist the normative blackmail of the reigning political imaginary, which imbues us with a meta-normative reflex to unconditionally accept democracy (which has become quite simply the indispensable name for the political good), it was not enough here to call into question the problematic role of this value-concept and to dissect its theodicy and the triumphalist historiography of its progress, which is supposed to be *our* progress. It was equally important to excavate the conceptual framework that subtends the idea according to which there could be a unique and ideal form of government *in general*. For it is the purity of the political—whether in the form of a distinct practice built upon a tabula rasa, of an autonomous sphere in the social world, or of a rarefied idea of something to come—which lies at the heart of the presupposition that there is a political good par excellence or a definitive form of government. As deceptive as it may be for all of those who have delighted in the epistemological utopia purporting to put an end to all other utopias, according to an absolute knowledge that has made "us" into the apotheosis of history, historical developments have no *eschaton,* and politics is without end. Democracy, whatever that means, will not save us from ourselves—from the collective task of the immanent elaboration of politics.

AFTERWORD

# Taking Charge of the Meanings and Directions of History

Man [ . . . ] has forgotten how to hope.
This hell of the present is at last his kingdom.
—Albert Camus

If there is not a single concept capable of capturing the specificity of the present, or of a significant subset thereof, it is because it is irreducible to a sole dimension or a unique trajectory. It has no single meaning or direction. There is, on the one hand, a plurality of significations and a multiplicity of methods for trying to grasp the present. This explains the importance of the notion of a historical imaginary, which is plural and varies according to time, space, and social milieu. On the other hand, history does not follow a sole and unique course, despite what some would have us believe. There are multiple directions and various currents. History is not to be confused with destiny, and one will not find a single motor at the core of all historical developments. There is rather a plurality of agencies that interact with one other in a highly complex chemistry. It is for this reason, among others, that the notion of a conjuncture is particularly pertinent, since it refers to the meeting point of multiple directions and meanings of history.

In proposing a counter-history of the present, this book does not seek to identify the characteristic feature of our time. On the contrary, it aims at breaking with epochal thought by highlighting the nonexistence of the present in the singular. Taking into account the three dimensions of history (time, space, society), it demonstrates that there is a plurality of presents. This is not only because every "present" is an enormous force field, a crossroads of different trajectories and significations, the site of several historical imaginaries (even if our conjuncture is marked by the overwhelming presence of a historico-political imaginary striving to impose a sole and unique meaning and direction on history). It is also because the "present" of a specific social space is not necessarily that of another social space. The counter-history outlined here is thus both a counter-geography and a counter-sociology. Whereas the dominant historical imaginary tries to flatten the world by homogenizing time, space, and society, I want to stress the radical variability of phenomena depending on their space-time and the sectors of society.

Yet this does not mean that our conjuncture loses all of its consistency (which is not the same thing as unicity). Indeed, one of the challenges of this book has been to propose a topological capture allowing us to elucidate the preponderant historical imaginary and dissect its theoretical foundations, while at the same time forging conceptual tools for an utterly different approach to the question of the present. Unlike epochal thought, a topological capture is always a reflexive construction, from a specific point of view, which proposes constellations in order to account for the broad outline of certain phenomena within a specific social space-time. It does not claim to identify the definitive nature of a period, but neither does it avoid participating in recognizable truth practices, precisely in order to try and displace or reconfigure images of the present time and the historical orders subtending them. The arguments regarding, for example, the ubiquity of oligarchy in the contemporary world should therefore not be taken as attempts to replace one epochal concept by another. This was, instead, an endeavor to provide an immanent analysis of democratic discourse in order to tease out the internal contradictions of actually existing democracy, while proposing a topological capture within the framework of a cartographic and stratigraphic elucidation.

This point is extremely important and applies equally to the chapters on technology and globalization. The key concepts that I have chosen to analyze here have certainly contributed in various ways, as we have seen, to the production of an image of the present according to which—to summarize briefly—we supposedly live in an age when the world is increasingly unified by a novel techno-economic network and an unprecedented democratic consensus. In dismantling this image piece by piece, the goal has not, however, been to oppose to it an antithetical history by suggesting, for instance, that reality is the opposite, or that there is no trace of such phenomena. It has rather been to propose a change in historical order in order to reconfigure everything and foreground, among other things, the chronological, geographic, and stratigraphic variability of the elements in question (which are, in effect, identifiable in certain strata of space-time). Furthermore, it was not enough to show the deep complicity between this image of the present and formidable political, economic, and social projects. It was also necessary to insist on the ways in which it tends to turn us into passive subjects, into spectators who would not dare try to change what imposes itself with the force of inevitability, while simultaneously removing any responsibility from those who contribute to the continuation or acceleration of the "crusade of popular capitalism" and all that it entails. This is not to mention the preservation of the status quo through a conservative blackmail according to which any effort to really change the course of history would inexorably lead to intolerable crimes.

This historico-political imaginary, as well as the order of history in which it is rooted, make us into true prisoners of our time. They produce a *sensus communis* of history by incarcerating us in a temporal order with no exit. To employ a slightly different vocabulary from the one used in the course of the preceding analyses, but one that has the advantage of concisely highlighting our historical captivity, we could say that the dominant historical imaginary is inhabited by a specific temporal apparatus (*dispositif*) that tends to orient it in a particular direction by transforming the present into the time of the now, the past into the ancient, and the future into what is to come (*le temps présent en temps-maintenant, le passé en l'ancien, et le futur en l'avenir*). Whereas one can understand the present as being deeply anchored in the past while constituting the chassis of experience in the moment, what I propose to call here the time of the now shakes off its historical inscription like an instantaneous flash that comes from nowhere. The now does not take place; it happens. Any investigation into its historical origins is blocked in advance by a *there is* without context: there is, for example, globalization, an unprecedented technological development, or a democratic consensus. Why inquire into the emergence of such ideas, or the ways in which they have favored—in their intertwining with various political, economic, social practices—the construction of an image of the present that has not at all been without effects? The past, in the apparatus of the time of the now, is in fact only the former or the ancient, namely what is behind us, old-fashioned, outdated, and uninteresting (or, in another variant, that which is but a preparatory step leading to contemporary reality or what is to come). We are thereby deprived of the ability to take charge of the past by elucidating the diverse ways in which what exists "now" is largely the nodal point, as complex as it is changing, of an extraordinary number of threads from the past. The ancient is only the dustbin of history where the refuse of past now-times accumulate, or indeed anything that has been condemned to it as if to a temporal tomb. We are hence delivered at the same time, so to speak, to what is to come, that is to say, to what happens to us, to what imposes itself on us (over which we have hardly any influence). By severing the ties between the past and the future, this temporal apparatus situates us within a horizon where it becomes impossible, in principle, to construct other futures by creating, step by step, and therefore in duration, worlds other than the one that comes at us.

The counter-history of the present undertaken here aims at freeing us from the shackles of the dehistoricized time of the now, where it goes without saying that we live and will live in a so-called global, technological, and democratic era. It proposes an alternative historical order allowing us to break with the dominant imaginary while taking charge of the present, as well as of the past and future, in the senses that I have indicated. This counter-history thereby seeks to create and render visible historical meanings and directions that radically challenge a very widespread image of our age. The present, anchored in the past as well as in social geography, takes on very different meanings (starting with the demolition of the very unity of "the present"). And the alleged direction of history toward an implacable future—destined to be nothing more than the incessant repetition, yet always more intense, of the time of the now—bursts open to make room for a field of struggles where multiple possible directions are at play. Far from preaching in the desert, this counter-history of the present endeavors to create zones of visibility and to give its full support to the various movements already under way, and for a long time, that strive to produce—and have really already produced—other historical meanings and directions. To advance further, by dismantling piece by piece a powerful historico-political imaginary, it attempts to open a breach in order to participate in the creation of a true future, that is a collective actualization of historical possibilities other than those that impose themselves on us by locking us within the intransigent destiny of what is to come (and must simply be undergone). Strictly speaking, counter-history is not only a history of the past and present that cuts against the grain. It is fundamentally a history of the future that aims at creating new historical meanings and directions (*de nouveaux sens historiques*), and thus quite simply new histories (*de nouvelles histoires tout court*). It is a matter, then, of nothing less than an effort to channel an expansive constellation of collective forces in order to contribute to changing the very significations and orientations of the story of time (*des sens mêmes de l'histoire*).

# NOTES

INTRODUCTION

1. In what follows, the expressions *political imaginary*, *historical imaginary*, and *historico-political imaginary* will be used to refer to a practical mode of intelligibility of politics and history. An imaginary, in this sense, is not simply phantasmagorical or a pure product of the imagination. It is also irreducible to classic conceptions of ideology, if they be representational, functional, or material. An imaginary is simultaneously theoretical and practical; it is a way of thinking that is also a way of being and acting. Furthermore, it traverses the various dimensions of social existence, including values, norms, affects, and representations. It is the ingrained modus operandi of social agents, which is part of interstitial cultural fabric rather than being imposed only from above or being purely subjective. This does not mean that it operates like an inescapable framework à la Pierre Macherey's "infra-ideology," but it does tend to function as a sociocultural given inscribed within the practical common sense of particular communities (see Pierre Macherey, *Le Sujet des normes* [Paris: Éditions Amsterdam, 2014]). It is not necessarily bounded, however, by the supposed horizons of specific societies or cultures. For an important and thoughtful debate on the category of the imaginary in contemporary social theory, which draws most notably on the work of Cornelius Castoriadis, Claude Lefort, Paul Ricœur, and Charles Taylor, see *Social Imaginaries* 1, no. 1 (2015).
2. On slums, see the 2003 United Nations report *The Challenge of the Slums*, as well as Mike Davis, "Planet of Slums," *New Left Review* 26 (March–April 2004). Regarding the global distribution of wealth, refer to Oxfam's recent report: "The gap between rich and poor is reaching new extremes. Crédit Suisse recently revealed that the richest 1% have now accumulated more wealth than the rest of the world put together. [ . . . ] Meanwhile, the wealth owned by the bottom half of humanity has fallen by a trillion dollars in the past five years. This is just the latest evidence that today we live in a world with levels of inequality we may not have seen for over a century. [ . . . ] In 2015, just 62 individuals had the same wealth as 3.6 billion

people—the bottom half of humanity" (Oxfam, "An Economy for the 1%," January 19, 2016, https://www.oxfam.org/sites/www.oxfam.org/files/file_attachments/bp210-economy-one-percent-tax-havens-180116-en_0.pdf>, accessed January 20, 2016).
3. ICT (International Telecommunication Union), "ICT Facts and Figures—The World in 2015": http://www.itu.int/en/ITU-D/Statistics/Documents/facts/ICTFactsFigures2015.pdf (accessed January 1, 2016).
4. See William Blum, *America's Deadliest Export: Democracy and the Truth about US Foreign Policy and Everything Else* (London: Zed Books, 2013), 1.
5. This coherence is multidimensional, but Lisa Gitelman has perfectly summarized one aspect of it in her critique of the history of technology and, by extension, of its intertwining relationship to a theodicy of globalization and representative democracy: "Today, the imagination of that end point [of media history] in the United States remains uncritically replete with confidence in liberal democracy, and has been most uniquely characterized by the cheerful expectation that digital media are all converging toward some harmonious combination or global 'synergy,' if not also toward some perfect reconciliation of 'man' and machine" (*Always Already New: Media, History, and the Data of Culture* [Cambridge, MA: MIT Press, 2006], 3).
6. It could be tempting to cite as a counter-example global warming or other changes that affect planet Earth as a whole. This is indeed a question of the utmost importance that must play a major role in the counter-history of the present (particularly because of all the forces who are still bent on concealing the devastating effects of the dominant economic model). Nevertheless, the impacts of such changes vary significantly based on location and social strata, and this is precisely one of the political issues at stake in the ecological struggle (brilliantly illustrated by the government of the Maldives when it held its cabinet meeting underwater). What is more, there is always a question of scale to be taken into account, and it should not be forgotten, in absolute terms, that such changes remain localized (in the broad sense of the term). Far from being limited to this planet and the anthropocentric framework, space extends, as far as we know, to infinity. This should not change anything regarding the ecological struggle, but it remains very important philosophically.
7. For a useful summary see, for example, the first pages of Geoffrey Pleyers, *Alter-Globalization: Becoming Actors in the Global Age* (Cambridge: Polity, 2010).
8. See Francis Fukuyama, *The End of History and the Last Man* (New York: Avon Books, 1992).

CHAPTER 1: A SPECTER IS HAUNTING GLOBALIZATION

This chapter was translated by Emily Rockhill in close consultation with the author.

1. Karl Marx, *The Eighteenth Brumaire of Louis Bonaparte* (New York: International Publishers, 1963), 15. On the theme of haunting and even a certain "hauntology," see Jacques Derrida, *Specters of Marx: The State of the Debt, the*

*Work of Mourning and the New International*, trans. Peggy Kamuf (New York: Routledge, 2006).

2. ICT (International Telecommunication Union), "ICT Facts and Figures—The World in 2015": http://www.itu.int/en/ITU-D/Statistics/Documents/facts/ICTFactsFigures2015.pdf (accessed January 1, 2016).

3. See Paul Hirst and Grahame Thompson, eds., *Globalization in Question* (Cambridge: Polity, 1999), and Serge Cordellier, ed., *La mondialisation au-delà des mythes* (Paris: La Découverte, 1997).

4. See David Harvey's conclusions in *A Brief History of Neoliberalism* (Oxford: Oxford University Press, 2005), 118–19.

5. See, for instance, Will Kymlicka's brief summary in "The New Debate on Minority Rights (and Postscript)," in *Multiculturalism and Political Theory*, ed. Anthony Simon Laden and David Owen (Cambridge: Cambridge University Press, 2007), 26.

6. See Davis, "Planet of Slums."

7. On this point, see Joseph Stiglitz, *Globalization and Its Discontents* (New York: W. W. Norton, 2002); Harvey, *A Brief History of Neoliberalism*; and John Perkins, *Confessions of an Economic Hit Man* (New York: Plume, 2006).

8. Eric Hobsbawm, *Globalization, Democracy and Terrorism* (London: Abacus, 2007), 110.

9. Jean-Jacques Rousseau, *Discours sur l'origine et les fondements de l'inégalité parmi les hommes / Discours sur les sciences et les arts* (Paris: Garnier-Flammarion, 1992), 190; J. G. Herder, *Philosophical Writings*, ed. and trans. Michael N. Forster (Cambridge: Cambridge University Press, 2002), 325, translation slightly modified.

10. As we will see, the "hyperglobalizers" and the "transformationalists" say "yes" and the "skeptics" say "no."

11. See René Dagorn, "Une brève histoire du mot 'mondialisation,'" in *Mondialisation: Les mots et les choses*, ed. GEMDEV (Paris: Éditions Karthala, 1999), 189.

12. On this issue, see Roland Robertson, *Globalization: Social Theory and Global Culture* (London: Sage, 1992).

13. Search for the term *globalization* in the *New York Times*, performed on January 1, 2016.

14. Search for the term *globalization* in *LexisNexis*, the *Washington Post*, and the *Los Angeles Times*, performed on January 1, 2016.

15. Frédéric Lebaron, *Le savant, le politique et la mondialisation* (Bellecombe-en-Bauges, France: Éditions du Croquant, 2003), 7.

16. Regarding this point, see Immanuel Wallerstein, "After Developmentalism and Globalization, What?," *Social Forces* 83, no. 3 (March 2005): 1263–78; Immanuel Wallerstein, *World-Systems Analysis: An Introduction* (Durham, NC: Duke University Press, 2004); and Ronaldo Munck, "Neoliberalism, Necessitarianism and Alternatives in Latin America: There Is No Alternative (TINA)?," *Third World Quarterly* 24, no. 3 (June 2003): 495–511.

17. On the purely ideological aspects of the Cold War, see Noam Chomsky, *Deterring Democracy* (New York: Hill and Wang, 1991), particularly the first chapter, titled "Cold War: Fact and Fancy."
18. Michael Mann emphasizes the importance of these two geopolitical events in his article "Has Globalization Ended the Rise and Rise of the Nation-State?," in *The Global Transformations Reader: An Introduction to the Globalisation Debate*, ed. David Held and Anthony McGrew (Cambridge: Polity, 2003), particularly 138. Let us note in passing that the hackneyed refrains of a certain neoliberal discourse ("democracy," "freedom," "equality," etc.) should not make us lose sight—this is precisely one of its objectives—of the distance between proclaimed values and actual values.
19. Milton Friedman, *Capitalism and Freedom* (Chicago: University of Chicago Press, 1982), 9.
20. I have borrowed the term *practico-inert* from Jean-Paul Sartre's *Critique de la raison dialectique*, vol. 1 (Paris: Éditions Gallimard, 1960), although I am not using it in strict conformity with his thought.
21. This is not the place to enter into the debate—marked most notably by the positions forcefully staked out by Cornelius Castoriadis and Louis Althusser—on the relationship between Marx's texts and the diverse social and historical practices that have tried to put them into practice.
22. In a very important variation on this first thesis, Francis Fukuyama has proposed a merger between Marx and Hegel by linking economic determinism to what he calls the desire for recognition. This desire, the "motor of history," is what purportedly allows him to combine the evolution of the free market economy with the development of "liberal" politics in a universal history of the progress of humanity, finally arriving at "the Promised Land" (Fukuyama, *The End of History*, xix, xv). Also see his lecture "The End of History Revisited," presented to the Long Now Foundation in San Francisco on June 28, 2007, where he affirms that science and technology constitute the veritable engine of history, connected by a "drive shaft" to economic development, which is then attached by a "loose set of connecting rods" to politics, and finally by weaker and weaker links to culture: http://fora.tv/2007/06/28/Francis_Fukuyama _End_Of_History_Revisited#%20 (accessed January 1, 2016).
23. "The main idea [*idée-force*] of the consensus," Jacques Rancière aptly writes in *La haine de la démocratie*, "is in effect that the global economic movement attests to a historical necessity to which we must adapt ourselves, and that the only ones capable of denying this are representatives of archaic interests and outmoded ideologies. Now this is also the idea that grounds their conviction and their science. They believe in progress. They had faith in the movement of history when it was leading to the worldwide socialist revolution. They still have faith now that it is leading to the global triumph of the market. It's not their fault if history made a mistake" (Jacques Rancière, *La haine de la démocratie* [Paris: Éditions La Fabrique, 2006], 94).
24. Marx, *The Eighteenth Brumaire*, 15.

25. Marx, *The Eighteenth Brumaire*, 15.
26. See Zygmunt Bauman, *Globalization: The Human Consequences* (New York: Columbia University Press, 1998), 59: "The deepest meaning conveyed by the idea of globalization is that of the indeterminate, unruly and self-propelled character of world affairs; the absence of a centre, of a controlling desk, of a board of directors, of a managerial office."
27. Richard Sanders, "GATS: The End of Democracy?" *Australian Financial Review*, June 15, 2001, http://australiatoday.webs.com/documents/GATS_End_of_Democracy_Sanders01.pdf. Also see Ernesto Laclau and Chantal Mouffe, *Hegemony and Socialist Strategy* (London: Verso, 2001), xvi: "Presented as driven exclusively by the information revolution, the forces of globalization are detached from their political dimensions and appear as a fate to which we all have to submit."
28. Cornelius Castoriadis, *Postscript on Insignificance: Dialogues with Cornelius Castoriadis*, ed. Gabriel Rockhill, trans. Gabriel Rockhill and John V. Garner (London: Continuum, 2011), 10.
29. Martin Wolf, "Keynes Offers Us the Best Way to Think about the Financial Crisis," *Financial Times*, December 23, 2008, http://www.ft.com/intl/cms/s/0/be2dbf2c-d113-11dd-8cc3-000077b07658.html#axzz3w8TtuFiG (accessed January 1, 2016).
30. Wolf, "Keynes Offers Us the Best Way to Think about the Financial Crisis."
31. Marc-Olivier Padis, "Introduction: Entre néolibéralisme et régulation. L'État à la croisée des chemins," *Esprit* 349 (November 2008): 7, 6.
32. She made this claim in a lecture at the University of Chicago, which was broadcast on October 6, 2008, and is available at http://www.democracynow.org/2008/10/6/naomi_klein (accessed January 1, 2016).
33. I would like to highlight in passing a major event that was largely effaced—and for good reason—by the financial storm: the bill authorizing, on September 24, 2008, $612 billion in military expenditures (see Chalmers Johnson, "We Have the Bailout Money—We're Spending It on War," *The Nation* [September 29, 2008]).
34. In the long list of important sources on these events, see the following: the interviews conducted by Amy Goodman with Adrienne Kinne (May 13, 2008), Mark Klein (July 7, 2008), and James Bamford (October 14, 2008) for *Democracy Now!*, http://www.democracynow.org; James Bamford, "The Spy Factory," PBS, February 3, 2009, http://www.pbs.org/wgbh/nova/spyfactory/program.html; the Amnesty International report "USA: Below the Radar: Secret Flights to Torture and 'Disappearance,'" April 4, 2006, https://www.amnesty.org/en/documents/AMR51/051/2006/en/; Witness, "Outlawed: Extraordinary Rendition, Torture and Disappearances in the 'War on Terror'": http://hub.witness.org/en/Outlawed (accessed January 1, 2016); two reports by the Council of Europe: "Allégations de détentions secrètes et de transferts interétatiques illégaux de détenus concernant des Etats membres du Conseil de l'Europe" (June 12, 2006) and "Détentions secrètes et transferts illégaux

de détenus impliquant des Etats membres du Conseil de l'Europe" (June 11, 2007); Dana Priest, "Wrongful Imprisonment: Anatomy of a CIA Mistake," *Washington Post*, December 4, 2005; Congressional Research Service Report for Congress, "Renditions: Constraints Imposed by Laws on Torture," October 12, 2007; Richard Clarke, *Against All Enemies: Inside America's War on Terror* (New York: Free Press, 2004); and Chisun Lee, "Bush's Secret Counterterrorism Law Book—and the Demands to Release It," *ProPublica*, January 28, 2009, http://www.propublica.org/article/obama-inherits-bushs-secret-counterterrorism-law-book-and-the-demands-to-re (accessed January 1, 2016).

35. On this issue, I refer the reader to a very interesting article on Obama's recovery plan, which has the distinct advantage of calling into question the naturalization of the economy, i.e., the procedure by which the economy is transformed into an uncontrollable natural force that necessarily and inevitably follows its own proper laws: Michael Hudson, "Obama's Awful Financial Recovery Plan," *CounterPunch*, February 12, 2009. Hudson underscores, moreover, the essential links between the contemporary financial situation and the history of economic and legislative decisions, recalling most notably the importance of the repeal of the Glass-Steagall Act in 1999, celebrated and embraced by Larry Summers, the former secretary of the treasury and director of the National Economic Council (See "Clinton Signs Legislation Overhauling Bank Laws," *New York Times*, November 13, 1999).

36. See Held and McGrew, *The Global Transformations Reader*. In taking Held and McGrew's arguments as a reference point, it is not my intention to criticize them or accept them as is. I am using them in a purely heuristic fashion without examining here the limits of their approach or the accuracy of their interpretations of the various authors cited.

37. See Held and McGrew, *The Global Transformations Reader*, 4–6.

38. See Held and McGrew, *The Global Transformations Reader*, 5: "Frequently associated with this skeptical position is a strong attachment either to an essentially Marxist or to a realist ontology."

39. It is important to emphasize that it is a question of tendencies rather than absolute principles. It is worth reviewing, in this regard, all of the examples cited in the introduction by David Held, Anthony McGrew, David Goldblatt, and Jonathan Perraton to *Global Transformations: Politics, Economics and Culture* (Stanford, CA: Stanford University Press, 1999), particularly 3, 5, 7, 11–12.

40. Anthony Giddens, *The Consequences of Modernity* (Stanford, CA: Stanford University Press, 1990), 55–63.

41. Giddens, *The Consequences of Modernity*, 63; see also 64.

42. See, for instance, Held et al., *Global Transformations*, 25–26.

43. It is not unimportant that Giddens began working on *The Consequences of Modernity* (1990) in the spring of 1988. It is worth noting, moreover, that he asserts that globalization is "a term which must have a key position in the lexicon of the social sciences" (*The Consequences of Modernity*, 52).

44. On this issue, see Justin Rosenberg's critique in *The Follies of Globalisation Theory* (London: Verso, 2002).
45. I will not dwell here on the differences that would need to be highlighted between this conception of ideology and the one found in Marx's early writings. I will simply limit myself to referring the interested reader to the third chapter of Étienne Balibar's excellent book *La philosophie de Marx* (Paris: Éditions La Découverte, 2001) as well as to the key texts by Marx and Engels, such as *The German Ideology*.
46. Pierre Bourdieu demonstrated this aspect of political imaginaries in "Le mythe de la 'mondialisation' et l'État social européen": "This kind of symbolic drip feed that written and televisual reporting contributes to so steadily—to a large extent unconsciously, because the majority of people who repeat these utterances do it in good faith—, produces profound effects. This is how, at the end of the day, neoliberalism presents itself under the appearance of *inevitability*" (*Contre-feux* [Paris: Éditions Raisons d'Agir, 1998], 35). Also see his article with Loïc Wacquant, "NewLiberalSpeak: Notes on the New Planetary Vulgate," trans. David Macey, *Radical Philosophy* 105 (January–February 2001) (this is a modified version of an article published in *Le monde diplomatique* in May 2000).
47. On this point, see Cornelius Castoriadis, *The Imaginary Institution of Society*, trans. Kathleen Blamey (Cambridge, MA: MIT Press, 1987), 39–40.
48. Thomas Kuhn, *The Essential Tension* (Chicago: University of Chicago Press, 1977), 309.
49. We could also invoke *linguistic criticism* and what Herbert Marcuse described as the "linguistic therapy" necessary to break with the common lexis that serves to maintain the status quo (see most notably *An Essay on Liberation* [Boston: Beacon, 1969]). This form of critique is obviously already at work in the analysis undertaken here.
50. Karl Marx, "A Letter on Russia," *New International* 1, no. 4 (November 1934): 110.
51. This article, published in *Socialisme ou Barbarie* between April 1964 and June 1965, was included in *The Imaginary Institution of Society*. With extremely different objectives, Hannah Arendt also called into question historical determinism and the idea that history is structured by laws or by regular movements such as the dialectic (see *Between Past and Future* [New York: Penguin, 1968], 79).
52. Castoriadis, *The Imaginary Institution of Society*, 23, translation slightly modified (also see 17). Raymond Williams formulated a similar argument in *Television: Technology and Cultural Form* (New York: Routledge, 2003).
53. Castoriadis, *The Imaginary Institution of Society*, 44–45, translation slightly modified.
54. Castoriadis, *The Imaginary Institution of Society*, 56.
55. See, for example, the accounts provided in Samir Amin, *Capitalism in the Age of Globalization: The Management of Contemporary Society*

(London: Zed Books, 2014); Stiglitz, *Globalization and Its Discontents*; Harvey, *A Brief History of Neoliberalism*; and David Harvey, *Spaces of Global Capitalism: Towards a Theory of Uneven Geographical Development* (London: Verso, 2006). Also see the detailed and captivating critique presented by John Perkins in *Confessions of an Economic Hit Man*.

56. Karl Polanyi, *The Great Transformation* (Boston: Beacon, 1944), 149.
57. Polanyi, *The Great Transformation*, 149.
58. Polanyi, *The Great Transformation*, 140. Also see 139: "There was nothing natural about *laissez-faire*; free markets could never have come into being merely by allowing things to take their course."
59. Polanyi, *The Great Transformation*, 57. Regarding the role of economism in Polanyi's book, it is worth noting that rather than a simple economic determinism, he invokes an economic determinism deduced from his own object of analysis, that is the economism proper to the era of laissez-faire economics.
60. Polanyi, *The Great Transformation*, 141. Pierre Bourdieu's critique of globalization acts as an interesting echo to Polanyi's thesis: "Economic 'globalization' is not a mechanical effect of the laws of technology or the economy but the product of a policy implemented by a set of agents and institutions, and the result of the application of rules deliberately created for specific ends;" Bourdieu, *Firing Back: Against the Tyranny of the Market 2*, trans. Loïc Wacquant (London: Verso, 2003), 84, translation slightly modified; *Contre-feux 2: Pour un mouvement social européen* (Paris: Éditions Raisons d'Agir, 2001), 95).

CHAPTER 2: ARE WE REALLY LIVING IN A TECHNOLOGICAL ERA?
Translated by John V. Garner in close consultation with the author.

1. On this issue, it is worth citing Bernard Stiegler's thesis, which is summarized in *Philosopher par accident: Entretiens avec Elie During* (Paris: Éditions Galilée, 2004), 83: "The *properly mnemotechnical* tertiary retentions, that Plato would speak of as hypomnesical, have controllable effects, and when these mnemotechniques are *orthothetical*, they open the age of history, of law, of philosophy, of science, and finally of what one calls the West. [ . . . ] My thesis is that the analogical and digital orthotheses proper to our time open another age, and my hypothesis is that this age is probably that of the end of the West."
2. On the three dimensions of history, I take the liberty of referring the reader to my book *Logique de l'histoire: Pour une analytique des pratiques philosophiques* (Paris: Éditions Hermann, 2010).
3. Stiegler, *Philosopher par accident*, 25 (my emphasis). Vilém Flusser gives himself over just as much to monolithic (though "hypothetical") positions, as for instance in *Towards a Philosophy of Photography* (London: Reaktion Books, 2000), 7: "The book is based on the hypothesis that two fundamental turning points can be observed in human culture since its inception. The first, around the middle of the second millennium BC, can be summed up under the heading 'the invention of linear writing'; the second, the one we are currently experiencing, could be called 'the invention of technical images.'"

4. Gilles Deleuze, *Negotiations: 1972–1990*, trans. Martin Joughin (New York: Columbia University Press, 1995), 180, 182 (translation slightly modified).
5. Deleuze, *Negotiations: 1972–1990*, 180, translations slightly modified.
6. Deleuze, *Negotiations: 1972–1990*, 181, 180, translations slightly modified.
7. See the report by the parliamentary commission of inquiry number 449 (1999–2000) by Jean-Jacques Hyest and Guy-Pierre Cabanel, filed on June 29, 2000, under the title "Les conditions de détention dans les établissements pénitentiaires en France," http://www.senat.fr/rap/l99-449/l99-449.html (accessed January 1, 2016).
8. Didier Fassin quite rightly speaks of a veritable "punitive turn" in the second half of the twentieth century. See, for instance, the discussion of his book *L'ombre du monde: Une anthropologie de la condition carcérale* (Paris: Éditions du Seuil, 2015) in the first part of the following broadcast: http://www.franceculture.fr/emission-la-suite-dans-les-idees-entre-les-murs-anthropologie-de-la-condition-carcerale-2015-01-03 (accessed January 1, 2016).
9. On this topic, I highly recommend Michelle Alexander, *The New Jim Crow: Mass Incarceration in the Age of Colorblindness* (New York: New Press, 2010).
10. ICT (International Telecommunication Union), "ICT Facts and Figures—The World in 2015": http://www.itu.int/en/ITU-D/Statistics/Documents/facts/ICTFactsFigures2015.pdf (accessed January 1, 2016).
11. ICT, "ICT Facts and Figures."
12. ICT, "ICT Facts and Figures."
13. ICT, "ICT Facts and Figures."
14. Cornelius Castoriadis, *The Imaginary Institution of Society*, trans. Kathleen Blamey (Cambridge, MA: MIT Press, 1987), 37.
15. See, for instance, David Harvey, *Spaces of Global Capitalism: A Theory of Uneven Geographical Development* (London: Verso, 2006).
16. Samir Amin, *Spectres of Capitalism: A Critique of Current Intellectual Fashions* (New York: Monthly Review Press, 1998), 19.
17. Janet Abbate, *Inventing the Internet* (Cambridge, MA: MIT Press, 1999), 4.
18. James Curran, Natalie Fenton, and Des Freedman, *Misunderstanding the Internet* (New York: Routledge, 2012), 9.
19. Curran, Fenton, and Freedman, *Misunderstanding the Internet*, 181.
20. Jacques Rancière, *The Politics of Aesthetics: The Distribution of the Sensible*, ed. and trans. Gabriel Rockhill (New York: Continuum, 2004), 33.
21. On this point, see the excellent book by Lisa Gitelman, *Always Already New: Media, History, and the Data of Culture* (Cambridge, MA: MIT Press, 2006).
22. Murray Bookchin, *Social Ecology and Communalism* (Oakland: AK Press, 2007), 19; Murray Bookchin, *Ecology and Revolutionary Thought* (New York: Times Change Press, 1970), 41. It is in the latter work that Bookchin appeals to the creation of ecotechnologies: "What is clearly needed is [ ... ] a reordering and redevelopment of technologies according to ecologically sound principles. We need an ecotechnology that will help harmonize society

with the natural world" (41). On this subject, see also "Towards a Liberatory Technology," in *Post-Scarcity Anarchism* (Palo Alto, CA: Ramparts, 1971), 83–140.
23. Raymond Williams, *Television: Technology and Cultural Form* (New York: Routledge, 2003), 133.
24. Cornelius Castoriadis, *The Imaginary Institution of Society*, trans. Kathleen Blamey (Cambridge, MA: MIT Press, 1987), 17, 23, translation slightly modified. See also Castoriadis, *Crossroads in the Labyrinth*, trans. Kate Soper and Martin H. Ryle (Cambridge, MA: MIT Press, 1984), 245: "But the technical ensemble itself lacks any meaning, technical or otherwise, if it is separated from the economic and social ensemble." Raymond Williams formulated a very similar argument in *Television*.
25. Stiegler, *Philosopher par accident*, 25.
26. Stiegler, *Philosopher par accident*, 64 (Stiegler's emphasis).
27. See Rockhill, *Logique de l'histoire*, 117–92.
28. See Eric Alfred Havelock, *Preface to Plato* (Cambridge, MA: Belknap Press of Harvard University Press, 1963); E. A. Havelock, "The Evidence for the Teaching Socrates," *Transactions and Proceedings of the American Philological Association* 65 (1934): 282–95; Jonathan Barnes, "The Hellenistic Platos," *Apeiron* 24, no. 2 (June 1991): 115–28.
29. Castoriadis, *Crossroads*, 230, translation slightly modified.
30. Andrew Feenberg, *Transforming Technology: A Critical Theory Revisited* (Oxford: Oxford University Press, 2002), 15.
31. *Charles Chaplin*, ed. Marcel Martin (Paris: Éditions Seghers, 1972), 145 (since I was unable to locate Chaplin's original English text, if there actually was one that was published, I have translated the quotations from this book in French into English). "A good silent picture," wrote Chaplin in his autobiography, "had universal appeal both to the intellectual and the rank and file. Now it was all to be lost" (*My Autobiography* [New York: Simon and Schuster, 1964], 325).
32. Martin, *Charles Chaplin*, 149.
33. Martin, *Charles Chaplin*, 149.
34. Martin, *Charles Chaplin*, 147.
35. For a more recent example, see the excellent article by Christian Christensen entitled "Wikileaks et les mythes de l'ère numérique" (*Le monde diplomatique* 678 [September 2010]: 23). By deconstructing the myth of the homogeneity of "social" media, as well as the myths of the disappearance of the nation-state and of the death of journalism, Christiensen demonstrates the specificity of WikiLeaks's approach to the management of information and of its political power. I would also direct the reader to the praiseworthy article by Edwy Plenel, "Nous sommes tous des WikiLeaks!" which in particular has the merit of insisting on the social inscription of new media: "Technology is not liberatory by its essence but by the social use one makes of it, the practices one promotes, the rights one wins, the resistances one organizes, in such a

way that it remains under the control of its users" (*Mediapart*, December 22, 2010, https://www.mediapart.fr/journal/international/221210/nous-sommes-tous-des-wikileaks). The Edward Snowden revelations, which I will briefly touch on in the following chapter, perfectly illustrate this idea.

CHAPTER 3: WHAT IS THE USE OF DEMOCRACY?

Translated by John V. Garner in close consultation with the author.

1. The relatively recent change that the category of enemy has undergone in the American political imaginary reveals the extent to which what is important is the form of opposition and its flexibility. Before, it was "communists" who were opposed to "democracy"; today it is "terrorists" and "tyrants" (see *The National Security Strategy of the U.S.A.*).

2. See John G. Neihardt, *Black Elk Speaks: The Complete Edition* (Lincoln: University of Nebraska Press, 2014).

3. We should reread in this light Frederick Douglass's overt interrogation—the importance of which cannot be overestimated—into the discrepancy between the stated ideals of the American Republic and its real practices. To the question, "What, to the American slave, is your 4th of July?" he firmly responded: "[A] day that reveals to him, more than all other days in the year, the gross injustice and cruelty to which he is the constant victim. To him, your celebration is a sham; your boasted liberty, an unholy license; your national greatness, swelling vanity; your sounds of rejoicing are empty and heartless; your denunciations of tyrants, brass fronted impudence; your shouts of liberty and equality, hollow mockery; your prayers and hymns, your sermons and thanksgivings, with all your religious parade, and solemnity, are, to him, mere bombast, fraud, deception, impiety, and hypocrisy—a thin veil to cover up crimes which would disgrace a nation of savages. There is not a nation on the earth guilty of practices, more shocking and bloody, than are the people of these United States, at this very hour. [ . . . ] [For] revolting barbarity and shameless hypocrisy, America reigns without a rival" (Frederick Douglass, *Selected Speeches and Writings*, ed. Philip S. Foner [Chicago: Lawrence Hill, 1999], 196–97).

4. See, for example, the excellent lecture presented by Maria Deraismes in 1870 entitled "La femme dans la démocratie [Woman in Democracy]." She makes a distinction in this text between democracy, which is naturally supportive of women, and the democrats, who are firmly opposed to them. By drawing up a balance sheet of democratization efforts, in particular with respect to those around 1789 and 1848 in France, she reaches an important conclusion concerning the way in which democrats conceive of universality (particularly with respect to the "universal suffrage" decreed in 1848): "The democrats have created a universal for their own use, an unprecedented universal, a pocket-sized universal, which leaves half of humanity aside" (*Ce que veulent les femmes: Articles et conférences de 1869 à 1891* [Paris: Éditions Syros, 1980], 86).

5. This expression is found in a speech delivered by Margaret Thatcher to the Conservative Party Conference in 1986.
6. For an analysis of the historical emergence of the reference to the Greek origin of European culture, particularly in a philosophical context and in relation to the supposed Greek birth of philosophy, I take the liberty of referring the reader to my book *Logique de l'histoire: Pour une analytique des pratiques philosophiques* (Paris: Éditions Hermann, 2010).
7. Daniel Bensaïd, "Permanent Scandal," in Giorgio Agamben, Alain Badiou, Daniel Bensaïd, Wendy Brown, Jean-Luc Nancy, Jacques Rancière, Kristin Ross, and Slavoj Žižek, *Democracy in What State?*, trans. William McCuaig (New York: Columbia University Press, 2009), 17–18, translation slightly modified.
8. Arthur Rimbaud, "Democracy," in *Collected Poems* (Oxford: Oxford University Press), 309, translation slightly modified. The original French text reads as follows (Arthur Rimbaud, *Œuvres complètes*, ed. Antoine Adam [Paris: Éditions Gallimard, 1972], 153–54):

> Le drapeau va au paysage immonde, et notre patois étouffe le tambour. Aux centres nous alimenterons la plus cynique prostitution. Nous massacrerons les révoltes logiques.
> Aux pays poivrés et détrempés!—au service des plus monstrueuses exploitations industrielles ou militaires.
> Au revoir ici, n'importe où. Conscrits du bon vouloir, nous aurons la philosophie féroce; ignorants pour la science, roués pour le confort; la crevaison pour le monde qui va. C'est la vraie marche. En avant, route!

9. Fukuyama, *The End of History*, 45.
10. Fukuyama, *The End of History*, 43.
11. This section takes back up and deepens several arguments that I formulated in "La démocratie dans l'histoire des cultures politiques," in *Jacques Rancière ou la politique à l'œuvre*, ed. Jérôme Game and Aliocha Lasowski (Paris: Éditions Archives Contemporaines, series "Centre d'Études Poétiques," 2009), 55–71.
12. David Graeber, "There Never Was a West: or, Democracy Emerges from the Spaces in Between," in *Possibilities: Essays on Hierarchy, Rebellion, and Desire* (Oakland, CA: AK Press, 2007), 346.
13. Partha Chatterjee, *Lineages of Political Society* (New York: Columbia University Press, 2011), xi.
14. Frantz Fanon, *Toward the African Revolution: Political Essays*, trans. Haakon Chevalier (New York: Grove, 1967), 97.
15. See in particular Benjamin Isakhan and Stephen Stockwell, ed., *The Secret History of Democracy* (New York: Palgrave Macmillan, 2011); Amartya Sen, "Democracy and Its Global Roots," *New Republic*, October 6, 2003, 28–35; Amartya Sen, "Democracy as a Universal Value," *Journal of Democracy* 10, no. 3 (1999): 3–17. From a slightly different perspective, which could be qualified as more critical, see Fred Dallmayr, "Liberal Democracy and Its Critics: Some Voices from East and West," *Democratic Culture: Historical*

and *Philosophical Essays*, ed. Akeel Bilgrami (New York: Routledge, 2011), 1–22, and Jack Goody, *The Theft of History* (Cambridge: Cambridge University Press, 2007), 240–66.

16. Despite the numerous strengths of David Graeber's analysis, he purports to be able to isolate the essence of democracy—roughly the belief in equality—and to identify it as a characteristic feature of human intelligence in general (see *The Democracy Project: A History, a Crisis, a Movement* [London: Allen Lane, 2012], 183–84). One also finds the same problem in a slightly different form (due to the systematic valorization of the *between* as a space of human freedom) in an article that is nevertheless far from being unimportant: "There Never Was a West," 346.

17. The overwhelming reference to Athens has cast a shadow over the other Greek cities with popular or democratic regimes, such that those that were established "in Miletus, in Megara, in Samos, from the start of the 6th Century" according to Jacqueline de Romilly, *Problèmes de la démocratie grecque* (Paris: Éditions Hermann, 1975), 3.

18. I refer in particular to the praiseworthy articles by Benjamin Isakhan and Stephen Stockwell in *The Secret History of Democracy* (New York: Palgrave Macmillan, 2011), 19–48.

19. Anthony H. Birch, *The Concepts and Theories of Modern Democracy*, 45.

20. We know more about what some Athenians—those whose writings have survived—said about the practices of their era than about what the people of Athens effectively did, as Benjamin Isakhan rightly reminds us in "What Is So 'Primitive' about 'Primitive Democracy'? Comparing the Ancient Middle East and Classical Athens," in Isakhan and Stockwell, *The Secret History*, 19–34.

21. See Edmond Lévy, *La Grèce au Ve siècle: De Clisthène à Socrate* (Paris: Éditions du Seuil, 1997), 128, and Antony Black, *A World History of Ancient Political Thought* (Oxford: Oxford University Press, 2009), 141.

22. See Arlene W. Saxonhouse, "Athenian Democracy: Modern Mythmakers and Ancient Theorists," *PS: Political Science and Politics* 26, no. 3 (September 1993): 486, and Moses Finley, *Politics in the Ancient World* (Cambridge: Cambridge University Press, 1983), 73.

23. On this point, consult Pierre Lévêque and Pierre Vidal-Naquet, *Cleisthenes the Athenian: An Essay on the Representation of Space and Time in Greek Political Thought from the End of the Sixth Century to the Death of Plato*, trans. David A. Curtis (New York: Prometheus, 1996), 7, 21–22, as well as Lévy, *La Grèce au Ve siècle*, 196.

24. On the numerous differences between Athenian democracy and modern democracy, refer to the following works: Moses I. Finley, *Democracy Ancient and Modern* (New Brunswick, NJ: Rutgers University Press, 1985); Moses I. Finley, *Ancient Slavery and Modern Ideology* (Princeton, NJ: Markus Wiener, 1998); Lévy, *La Grèce V$^e$ siècle*; Pierre Vidal-Naquet, *Le chasseur noir: Formes de pensée et formes de société dans le monde grec* (Paris: Éditions

La Découverte, 2005); and Cornelius Castoriadis, *La montée de l'insignifiance* (Paris: Éditions du Seuil, 1996).

25. Finley, *Democracy Ancient and Modern*, 8–9.
26. Bertlinde Laniel, *Le mot "democracy" et son histoire aux États-Unis de 1780 à 1856* (Saint-Étienne, France: Publications de l'Université de Saint-Étienne, 1995), 47. See also Finley, *Democracy Ancient and Modern*, 9; Stephen R. Graubard, "Democracy," *Dictionary of the History of Ideas*, ed. Philip P. Wiener (New York: Charles Scribner's Sons, 1973), 652–67; R. R. Palmer, "Notes on the Use of the Word 'Democracy' 1789–1799," *Political Science Quarterly* 68, no. 2 (June 1953): 204; and John R. Wallach, "None of Us Is a Democrat Now," *Theory and Event* 13, no. 2 (2010).
27. Pierre Rosanvallon, "The History of the Word 'Democracy' in France," trans. Philip J. Costopoulous, *Journal of Democracy* 6, no. 4 (October 1995): 140–41. On this point, also consult Robert A. Dahl, *On Democracy* (New Haven, CT: Yale University Press, 2000), 7–9.
28. On this point, see Sheldon Wolin, *Democracy Incorporated: Managed Democracy and the Specter of Inverted Totalitarianism* (Princeton, NJ: Princeton University Press, 2010), 242.
29. John Locke, *Two Treatises of Government* (Cambridge: Cambridge University Press, 1988), 355.
30. See Mark Goldie, ed., *Locke: Political Essays* (Cambridge: Cambridge University Press, 1997), 160–62.
31. This is also the case, obviously, for Thomas Hobbes (1588–1679), who formulated by contrast an argued rejection of democracy as an unstable and fragile form of government.
32. See Andrew Sharp, ed., *The English Levellers* (Cambridge: Cambridge University Press, 1998).
33. On this point, it is helpful to consult David Wootton, "Leveller Democracy and the Puritan Revolution," in *The Cambridge History of Political Thought 1450–1700*, ed. J. H. Burns with Mark Goldie (Cambridge: Cambridge University Press, 2014), 412–42, and Andrew Sharp, introduction to *The English Levellers*, esp. xii–xiii, xxii.
34. William F. Swindler, ed., *Sources and Documents of United States Constitutions*, vol. 8 (Dobbs Ferry, NY: Oceana, 1979), 356.
35. Baruch Spinoza, *Theological-Political Treatise* (Cambridge: Cambridge University Press, 2007), 200.
36. See Jonathan Israel, "The Intellectual Origins of Modern Democratic Republicanism (1660–1720)," *European Journal of Political Theory* 3, no. 7 (2004): 7–36, and Jonathan Israel, *Radical Enlightenment* (Oxford: Oxford University Press, 2001). For an interesting exception in England, see the pro-democratic article by Sir William Petty (1623–87) published under the title "Petty *contra* Hobbes: A Previously Untranslated Manuscript," by Frank Amati and Tony Aspromourgos, *Journal of the History of Ideas* 46, no. 1 (January–March 1985): 127–32.

37. See Raymond Williams, *Culture and Society 1780–1950* (London: Penguin, 1961), 14.
38. Laniel, "*Le mot 'democracy*,'" 31.
39. Montesquieu, *The Spirit of the Laws*, trans. and ed. Anne M. Cohler, Basia Carolyn Miller, and Harold Samuel Stone (Cambridge: Cambridge University Press, 1989), 112.
40. See Montesquieu, *The Spirit of the Laws*, 114: "As far as the sky is from the earth, so far is the true spirit of equality from the spirit of extreme equality."
41. Montesquieu, *The Spirit of the Laws*, 159.
42. Montesquieu, *The Spirit of the Laws*, 160.
43. Jean-Jacques Rousseau, *Basic Political Writings*, trans. and ed. Donald A. Cress (Indianapolis: Hackett, 1987), 180. "Thus defined, the democracy of Montesquieu and Rousseau," writes Pierre Rosanvallon, "is at once an ideal type that can fit into an Aristotelian-style typology of political regimes and a historical model realized in a handful of ancient republics with strict moral standards. Yet neither of these two authors imagined that democracy could suit the modern world" ("History of the Word Democracy," 141).
44. Rousseau, *Basic Political Writings*, 180.
45. Rousseau, *Basic Political Writings*, 180.
46. Rousseau, *Basic Political Writings*, 180.
47. Rousseau, *Basic Political Writings*, 26.
48. Rousseau, *Basic Political Writings*, 28.
49. David Hume, *Selected Essays*, ed. Steven Copley and Andrew Edgar (Oxford: Oxford University Press, 1998), 28.
50. Giambattista Vico, *New Science*, trans. Dave Marsh (London: Penguin, 1999), 109.
51. Immanuel Kant, *Toward Perpetual Peace and Other Writings on Politics, Peace, and History*, trans. David L. Colclasure (New Haven, CT: Yale University Press, 2006), 76.
52. Kant, *Toward Perpetual Peace*, 74.
53. Ralph Louis Ketcham, ed., *The Anti-Federalist Papers and the Constitutional Convention Debates* (New York: Signet, 2003), 6. See also Alexander Hamilton's speech at the Federal Convention in 1787: "The members most tenacious of republicanism are as loud as any in declaiming against the vices of democracy" (John R. Vile, ed., *The Constitutional Convention of 1787: A Comprehensive Encyclopedia of America's Founding* [Santa Barbara, CA: ABC-CLIO, 2005], 896).
54. Clinton Rossiter, ed., *The Federalist Papers: Alexander Hamilton, James Madison, John Jay* (New York: Signet, 2003), 95.
55. Rossiter, *The Federalist Papers*, esp. 66–79.
56. Rossiter, *The Federalist Papers*, 69. See also Ketcham, *The Anti-Federalist*, 76–77. For other examples of the condemnation of democracy and of its comparison with anarchy and instability, see Robert W. Shoemaker, "'Democracy' and 'Republic' as Understood in Late Eighteenth-Century America," *American Speech* 41, no. 2 (May 1966): 83–95.

57. Cited in Laniel, *Le mot "democracy,"* 64–65.
58. See John Adams, *The Works of John Adams, Second President of the United States: With a Life of the Author, Notes and Illustrations*, vol. 6 (Boston: Charles C. Little and James Brown, 1851), 8–9. Alexander Hamilton made very similar comments at the Philadelphia Convention (see Max Farrand, ed., *The Records of the Federal Convention of 1787*, vol. 1 [New Haven, CT: Yale University Press, 1987], 299).
59. Adams, *The Works of John Adams*, 6:98.
60. Farrand, *The Records*, 1:26–27; see also 51, 48, 123, 132.
61. Farrand, *The Records*, 1:48.
62. This largely holds true as well for the establishment of the French republic, as we shall see. On the use of the term *democracy* in the language of the French Revolution, see Rosanvallon, "History of the Word," 142: "The ancient—and almost technical—connotations of the word 'democracy' in the 18th century explain why it was absent from the revolutionary discourse of 1789. The idea of a regime in which the people acted directly as legislator and magistrate in fact stirred no one, for it seemed to hark back to a bygone past, corresponding to an archaic and unstable stage of political life." The results of the lexicographic study conducted by Raymonde Monnier are at once telling and more precise in this respect. For in the Frantext database, "we find 258 occurrences [of the word *démocratie*] up until the Revolution (including 256 from 1740 to 1788), 91 uses of the word in the texts of the Revolution, 621 in the 19th century and more than double that in the 20th century. The progression is relatively similar for the adjective '*démocratique*'" (Raymonde Monnier, "Démocratie et Révolution française," *Mots* 59 [1999]: 50). The frequency of the word *démocratie* remains far behind the cherished terms of the Revolution, such as *souveraineté, peuple, liberté, nation, constitution, loi, patrie, république, citoyen* (Monnier, "Démocratie et Révolution française," 55).
63. Howard Zinn, *A People's History of the United States* (New York: HarperCollins, 2015), 96.
64. Herbert J. Storing, ed., *The Complete Anti-Federalist*, vol. 2 (Chicago: University of Chicago Press, 2008), 13. It is also worth consulting Terry Bouton, *Taming Democracy: "The People," the Founders, and the Troubled Ending of the American Revolution* (Oxford: Oxford University Press, 2007), 4.
65. Ketcham, *The Anti-Federalist*, 313. I take the liberty of referring the reader, in this regard, to the revealing description provided by Sheldon Wolin in *Democracy Incorporated*, 154–55.
66. Ketcham, *The Anti-Federalist*, 199. This is also largely the case in France, as Francis Dupuis-Déri has rightly recounted: "The republican elite thus emerged victorious from a bloody conflict: here a war of independence, there a revolution. In the United States as in France, this new elite did not associate itself with democracy and did not present the new regime as democratic" (Francis Dupuis-Déri, *Démocratie: Histoire politique d'un mot aux États-Unis et en France* [Montréal: Lux Éditeur, 2013], 305).

67. Ketcham, *The Anti-Federalist*, 199.
68. Thomas Paine, *Rights of Man* (New York: Dover, 1999), 114.
69. Dupuis-Déri, *Démocratie*, 293. See, for example, Robespierre's speech on February 5, 1794, in Richard Bienvenu, *The Ninth of Thermidor: The Fall of Robespierre* (Oxford: Oxford University Press, 1970), 32–49.
70. Alain Maillard, Claude Mazauric, and Eric Walter, ed., *Présence de Babeuf: Lumières, révolution, communism* (Paris: Publications de la Sorbonne, 1994), 254.
71. Graeber, *The Democracy Project*, 169.
72. Dupuis-Déri, *Démocratie*, 10; see also 357. In the meticulous study *Le mot "democratie,"* Bertlinde Laniel highlights another aspect of this change: "Liberated form the stigma of chronic political instability (democracy does not mean anarchy), democracy is not only interpreted in a political and social sense as a form of regime implying the natural right of people to politically participate in the name of their own proper interests, but as an ideal, even as an ideology. [ . . . ] In the course of the 19th century, the political, constitutional, meaning of democracy as a political regime among others increasingly disappears in the face of social (majority rule) and ideological significations (*democratic* justice and virtue are the ultimate objectives of political life)" (205).
73. Auguste Blanqui, "Lettre à Maillard," June 6, 1852, *Textes choisis* (Paris: Éditions Sociales, 1971), 131.
74. Rosanvallon, "The History of the Word," 144.
75. Rosanvallon, "The History of the Word," 140, translation slightly modified.
76. Alexis de Tocqueville, *Democracy in America*, trans. Henry Reeve (Washington, DC: Regnery, 2002), 5–6, translation slightly modified. The destruction of indigenous peoples was supposedly dictated by God, apparently so that equality could be spread through Christendom (see de Tocqueville, *Democracy in America*, 20).
77. Kristin Ross, "Democracy for Sale," in Agamben et al., *Democracy in What State?*, 90.
78. Ross, "Democracy for Sale," 95–96.
79. It is very important in this respect that contemporary democratophilia has forged an entire historical mythology around the development of democracy, and particularly around its Athenian golden age. See on this point Martin Bernal, *Black Athena: The Afroasiatic Roots of Classical Civilization*, vol. 1, *The Fabrication of Ancient Greece 1785–1985* (New Brunswick, NJ: Rutgers University Press, 1987), and Saxonhouse, "Athenian Democracy."
80. Walt Whitman, *The Works of Walt Whitman* (Ware, UK: Wordsworth Editions, 1995), 5.
81. See Walt Whitman, *Democratic Vistas and Other Papers* (Amsterdam: Fredonia Books, 2002), 62.
82. Whitman, *The Works*, 110. We should highlight in passing his reference to "the manly love of comrades," since Whitman's democracy is also a new social order that challenges—at least partially—heteronormativity.

83. Karl Polanyi, *The Great Transformation: The Political and Economic Origins of Our Time* (Boston: Beacon, 2001), 180. See also 234: "Inside and outside England, from Macaulay to Mises, from Spencer to Sumner, there was not a militant liberal who did not express his conviction that popular democracy was a danger to capitalism."
84. By way of illustration, see Karl Marx, *Critique of Hegel's "Philosophy of Right"* (1843; Cambridge: Cambridge University Press, 1982), and John Stuart Mill, *Considerations on Representative Government* (1861; Cambridge: Cambridge University Press, 2010).
85. V. I. Lenin, *The State and Revolution* (Chicago: Haymarket Books, 2014), 127–28.
86. Herbert Marcuse, *An Essay on Liberation* (Boston: Beacon, 1969), 59.
87. See for example Jean-Paul Sartre, *La responsabilité de l'écrivain* (Paris: Éditions Verdier, 1998), 39–40.
88. Alain Badiou, "The Democratic Emblem," in Agamben et al., *Democracy in What State?*, 6–7, translation slightly modified.
89. Laniel, *Le mot "démocracy,"* 31.
90. Rosanvallon, "History of the Word," 140.
91. Palmer, "Notes on the Use of the Word 'Democracy,'" 203.
92. Geraint Parry, *Political Elites* (London: George Allen and Unwin, 1969), 141.
93. Wendy Brown, "We Are All Democratic Now . . . ," in Agamben et al., *Democracy in What State?*, 44–45.
94. Eric Hobsbawm, *Globalisation, Democracy and Terrorism* (London: Abacus, 2007), 95. For Partha Chatterjee, modern democracy is founded on an even more universal basis, which is that of popular sovereignty as the principle of state legitimacy: "Even the most undemocratic of modern regimes must claim its legitimacy not from divine right or dynastic succession or the right of conquest but from the will of the people, however expressed. Autocrats, military dictatorships, one-party regimes—all rule, or so they must say, on behalf of the people" (Partha Chatterjee, *The Politics of the Governed: Reflections on Popular Politics in Most of the World* [New York: Columbia University Press, 2004], 27).
95. Wolin, *Democracy Incorporated*, 60.
96. Noam Chomsky, *Deterring Democracy* (New York: Hill and Wang, 1992), 331.
97. Chomsky, *Deterring Democracy*, 331.
98. Chomsky, *Deterring Democracy*, 331.
99. William Blum, *America's Deadliest Export: Democracy—The Truth about US Foreign Policy and Everything Else* (London: Zed Books, 2013), 1.
100. See Chomsky, *Deterring Democracy* and *The Chomsky Trilogy* (Tucson: Odonian, 1997), as well as works such as Greg Grandin, *Empire's Workshop: Latin America, the United States, and the Rise of the New Imperialism* (New York: Metropolitan Books, 2010), and John Perkins, *Confessions of an Economic Hit Man* (New York: Plume, 2006). As Michael Parenti explains in *Democracy for the Few*, 8th ed. (Boston: Thomson Wadsworth, 2008), with numerous

examples in support of his claim, "U.S. rulers mainly have been interested in defending the capitalist world from social change—even when the change has been peaceful and democratic" (85; see also 149–50).

101. Martin Luther King Jr., "A Time to Break Silence," in *A Testament of Hope: The Essential Writings and Speeches of Martin Luther King, Jr.* (New York: HarperCollins, 1986), 233.

102. Concentrating on the current era, Naomi Klein writes in *The Shock Doctrine*: "Since the fall of Communism, free markets and free people have been packaged as a single ideology that claims to be humanity's best and only defense against repeating a history filled with mass graves, killing fields and torture chambers. Yet in the Southern Cone, the first place where the contemporary religion of unfettered free markets escaped from the basement workshops of the University of Chicago and was applied in the real world, it did not bring democracy; it was predicated on the overthrow of democracy in country after country. And it did not bring peace but required the systematic murder of tens of thousands and the torture of between 100,000 and 150,000 people" (*The Shock Doctrine: The Rise of Disaster Capitalism* [New York: Picador, 2008], 102).

103. I would refer the reader on this point to Jeremy Scahill, *Blackwater: The Rise of the World's Most Powerful Mercenary Army* (New York: Nation Books, 2008).

104. See Human Rights Watch, *World Report 2014*, 642, http://www.hrw.org/world-report/2014 (accessed January 1, 2016).

105. Michelle Alexander, *The New Jim Crow: Mass Incarceration in the Age of Colorblindness* (New York: New Press, 2012), 1.

106. For an overview of the memorandums aiming to justify torture, see *New York Times*, "A Guide to the Memos on Torture," http://www.nytimes.com/ref/international/24MEMO-GUIDE.html (accessed January 1, 2016).

107. Concerning the assassination list and Obama's appalling statement that he is "really good at killing people," consult Mollie Reilly, "Obama Told Aides He's 'Really Good at Killing People,' New Book 'Double Down' Claims," *Huffington Post*, November 3, 2013, http://www.huffingtonpost.com/2013/11/03/obamadrones-double-down_n_4208815.html. The stances of the American administration on the revolutionary uprisings in the Mediterranean world are only the latest examples of the performative contradictions in its relation to democracy. See, for example, the excellent summary of the situation in Egypt offered by Chris Toensing in Ahdaf Soueif, "Amidst Egypt's Bloodshed, 'We Are Trying to Keep the Discourse of the Revolution Alive,'" *Democracy Now!*, August 19, 2013, http://www.democracynow.org/2013/8/19/ahdaf_soueif_amidst_egypts_bloodshed_we.

108. It should be noted that the principle of the separation of powers was defended in particular by anti-democrats like John Adams who aimed at separating and limiting the power of popular assemblies (in this case, the House of Representatives). As Alexander Hamilton explained so well: "There should be, in every republic, some permanent body to correct the prejudices,

[and] check the intemperate passions [ . . . ] of a popular assembly" (cited in Shoemaker, "'Democracy' and 'Republic,'" 93–94).
109. It is revealing in this respect that during the debate on federalism, Mr. Baldwin distinguished between the *"equality of men,"* on the one hand, and "the whole animal creation," on the other hand (Ketcham, *The Anti-Federalist*, 163).
110. See Bouton, *Taming Democracy*, as well as Shoemaker, "'Democracy' and 'Republic.'"
111. Parenti, *Democracy for the Few*, 154.
112. Nick Wing, "Jimmy Carter Defends Edward Snowden, Says NSA Spying Has Compromised Nation's Democracy," *Huffington Post*, July 18, 2013, http://www.huffingtonpost.com/2013/07/18/jimmy-carter-edward-snowden_n_3616930.html.
113. Glenn Greenwald, with Juan González, "Growing Backlash against NSA Spying Shows Why U.S. Wants to Silence Edward Snowden," *Democracy Now!*, July 18, 2013, http://www.democracynow.org/2013/7/18/glenn_greenwald_growing_backlash_against_nsa.
114. Bailey Cahall, David Sterman, Emily Schneider, and Peter Bergen, "Do NSA's Bulk Surveillance Programs Stop Terrorists?" January 13, 2014, http://www.newamerica.net/publications/policy/do_nsas_bulk_surveillance_programs_stop_terrorists. The metadata collected outside the United States and the metadata collected "under an unidentified authority" appear to have played an initiating role in the detection of a handful of other conspiracies.
115. See OccupyArrests.com's running total of the number of Occupy protestors arrested in the U.S., http://stpeteforpeace.org/occupyarrests.sources.html (accessed January 1, 2016) and Naomi Wolf, "The Shocking Truth about the Crackdown on Occupy," *The Guardian*, November 25, 2011, http://www.theguardian.com/commentisfree/cifamerica/2011/nov/25/shocking-truth-about-crackdown-occupy. On the profound differences between the prosecution of nonviolent protestors, and "the people" more generally, on the one hand, and the prosecution of the financial elite, on the other, it is helpful to consult the interview with Matt Taibbi about his book *The Divide: American Injustice in the Age of the Wealth Gap* (New York: Spiegel and Grau, 2014): Matt Taibbi, with Amy Goodman and Aaron Maté, "Who Goes to Jail?," *Democracy Now!*, April 15, 2014, http://www.democracynow.org/2014/4/15/who_goes_to_jail_matt_taibbi.
116. Wolin, *Democracy Incorporated*, 44. For another analysis of the de-democratization of contemporary democracy, see Wendy Brown's penetrating analysis in "We Are All Democrats Now."
117. Wolin, *Democracy Incorporated*, 239.
118. Wolin, *Democracy Incorporated*, 54–55.
119. Samir Amin rightly speaks of "everywhere, oligarchy" in "African Economist Samir Amin on the World Social Forum, Globalization and the Barbarism of Capitalism," *Democracy Now!*, March 27, 2015, http://www.democracynow.org/2015/3/27/african_economist_samir_amin_on_the.

120. Cornelius Castoriadis, *Post-Script on Insignificance*, trans. Gabriel Rockhill, John V. Garner, et al. (New York: Continuum, 2011), 7. On this point see also Castoriadis, "Done and to Be Done," in *The Castoriadis Reader*, trans. David A. Curtis (Oxford: Blackwell, 1997), 406–9.
121. Wolin, *Democracy Incorporated*, 212. It is also helpful to consult Wolin, *Democracy Incorporated*, 47, and Parenti, *Democracy for the Few*.
122. Ross, "Democracy for Sale," in Agamben et al., *Democracy in What State?*, 97; see also 98–99.
123. International Institute for Democracy and Electoral Assistance, http://www.idea.int/vt/countryview.cfm?id=231#pres (accessed January 1, 2016).
124. See the excellent article by Thomas A. Koelble and Edward Lipuma, "Democratizing Democracy: A Postcolonial Critique of Conventional Approaches to the 'Measurement of Democracy,'" *Democratization* 15, no. 1 (2008): 1–28.
125. See Ewan Robertson, "Former US President Carter: Venezuelan Electoral System 'Best in the World,'" *venezuelanalysis.com*, September 22, 2012, http://venezuelanalysis.com/news/7272.
126. Parenti, *Democracy for the Few*, 198.
127. Castoriadis, *Postscript on Insignificance*, 17.
128. "Public opinion," writes Castoriadis very insightfully, "has access to the information one wants to provide it with; it is manipulated in every way, and enormous effort has to be put into blocking out, periodically and only after the fact, a small part of what is perpetrated by the state, political, and economic bureaucratic apparatuses around the clock" (Cornelius Castoriadis, *Le monde morcelé: Les carrefours du labyrinth 3* [Paris: Éditions du Seuil, 1990], 102). Let us note in passing the flagrant exclusion of Dennis Kucinich—an American presidential candidate who was not entirely like the others—from the televised debate in Las Vegas on January 15, 2008. See Brian Stelter, "NBC Wins Battle over Debate," *New York Times*, January 15, 2008, http://thecaucus.blogs.nytimes.com/2008/01/15/nbc-wins-battle-overdebate/?_php=true&_type=blogs&_r=0. We should also mention the radical exclusion of advocates of the single-payer system in the healthcare debate organized by the Obama administration.
129. Cornelius Castoriadis, *Figures of the Thinkable*, trans. Helen Arnold (Stanford, CA: Stanford University Press, 2007), 125, translation slightly modified.
130. Erich Fromm, *The Sane Society* (New York: Routledge, 1956), 186.
131. According to Michael Parenti, "Money may not guarantee victory, but the lack of it usually guarantees defeat" (*Democracy for the Few*, 197). For political party expenditures since 2000, see the Center for Responsive Politics's overview, https://www.opensecrets.org/parties/index.php?cmte=&cycle=2014 (accessed January 1, 2016).
132. Russ Choma, "Millionaires' Club: For First Time, Most Lawmakers Are Worth $1 Million-Plus," *OpenSecrets Blog*, January 9, 2014, http://www.opensecrets.org/news/2014/01/millionaires-club-for-first-time-most-lawmakers-are-worth-1-million-plus.html.

133. John Nichols and Robert Waterman McChesney, *Dollarocracy: How the Money and Media Election Complex Is Destroying America* (New York: Nation Books, 2013), 6.
134. Martin Gilens and Benjamin I. Page, "Testing Theories of American Politics: Elites, Interest Groups, and Average Citizens," *Perspectives on Politics* 12, no. 3 (September 2014): 564–81 (I owe this reference to Avi Alpert). See also the following interview with Gilens: "Scholar behind Viral 'Oligarchy' Study Tells You What It Means," *Talking Points Memo*, April 22, 2014, http://talkingpointsmemo.com/dc/princeton-scholar-demise-of-democracy-america-tpm-interview.
135. See, for example, Philippe Rivière, "WikiLeaks, mort au messager," *Le monde diplomatique*, January 2011.
136. Parenti, *Democracy for the Few*, 193.
137. At the moment of its ratification, the anti-Federalist who wrote under the name of Brutus clearly identified this problem (see Ketcham, *The Anti-Federalist*, 329–30).
138. On this issue, it is worth consulting Parenti, *Democracy for the Few*, 188–209, as well as all of the reports on *Democracy Now!* concerning the numerous obstacles erected by the American government against the right to vote and the diverse attempts to overcome them: http://www.democracynow.org/topics/voting.
139. Parenti, *Democracy for the Few*, 198.
140. Rasmussen Reports, "35% Think U.S. Elections Are Fair," http://www.rasmussenreports.com/public_content/politics/general_politics/october_2013/35_think_u_s_elections_are_fair (accessed January 1, 2016).
141. Rasmussen Reports, "47% Think Neither Political Party Represents the American People," http://www.rasmussenreports.com/public_content/politics/general_politics/october_2013/47_think_neither_political_party_represents_the_american_people (accessed January 1, 2016), and Rasmussen Reports, "New High: 48% Say Most Members of Congress Are Corrupt," http://www.rasmussenreports.com/public_content/politics/general_politics/december_2011/new_high_48_say_most_members_of_congress_are_corrupt (accessed January 1, 2016). See also Rasmussen Reports, "Congressional Performance," http://www.rasmussenreports.com/public_content/politics/mood_of_america/congressional_performance (accessed January 1, 2016), and the following Gallup polls: http://www.gallup.com/poll/165392/perceived-need-third-party-reaches-new-high.aspx; http://www.gallup.com/poll/166244/americans-cite-gov-economy-healthcare-top-problems.aspx; http://www.gallup.com/poll/166844/government-itself-cited-top-problem.aspx (accessed January 1, 2016).
142. "Only 30% of Americans Trust Our Government," *Infowars*, March 12, 2013, http://www.infowars.com/only-30-of-americans-trust-our-government/.
143. Castoriadis, *Postscript on Insignificance*, 12.
144. Castoriadis, *Postscript on Insignificance*, 7. See also Akeel Bilgrami's argument concerning the epistemic deficiencies of the people in "Democracy and Disenchantment," *Social Scientist* 37, no. 11/12 (November–December 2009): 4–21.

145. Bensaïd, "Permanent Scandal," in Agamben et al., *Democracy in What State?*, 22. Castoriadis expresses a very similar opinion: "The postulate according to which *doxa*, opinion, is equally shared, is of course an entirely theoretical postulate. For this postulate to have a bit of substance, *doxa* must be cultivated" (Castoriadis, *Postscript on Insignificance*, 12).
146. Brown, "We Are All Democrats Now . . . ," 53.
147. According to Marcuse's analysis: "In the contemporary period, the questions as to the 'end of government' have subsided. It seems that the continued functioning of the society is sufficient justification for its legality and its claim for obedience, and 'functioning' seems defined rather negatively as absence of civil war, massive disorder, economic collapse. Otherwise anything goes: military dictatorship, plutocracy, government by gangs and rackets. Genocide, war crimes, crimes against humanity are not effective arguments against a government which protects property, trade, and commerce at home while it perpetrates its destructive policy abroad" (Marcuse, *An Essay on Liberation*, 67).
148. Although I cannot go into detail here, I would nevertheless like to briefly clarify this reference to the work of Jacques Derrida. The author of *Rogues* suggests that "'democracy to come' has to do neither with the *constitutive* (with what Plato would call the paradigmatic) nor with the *regulative* (in the Kantian sense of a regulative Idea)," even if he also admits that he does not vow to never give in to the regulative idea (*Rogues: Two Essays on Reason*, trans. Pascale-Anne Brault and Michael Naas [Stanford, CA: Stanford University Press, 2005], 31). "The 'to-come,'" he explains, "not only points to the promise but suggests that democracy will never exist, in the sense of a present existence: not because it will be deferred but because it will always remain aporetic in its structure" (86). The expression *democracy to come* therefore signals the urgency of bringing about the impossible, or what is at once the condition of possibility and of impossibility of politics (by which we should understand "true" politics). After all, democracy for Derrida is understood in the end as différance: "In both senses of différance, then, democracy is differential; it is *différance, renvoi*, and spacing" (38). It is a matter of the aporetic structure of political sense that calls us to do the impossible. Derrida's work is thus clearly inscribed within contemporary democratophilia, and it reproduces numerous aspects of the conventional and "occidentalist" history of democracy by tracing a largely linear and partially disincarnated trajectory from the Greeks to our present. He also maintains what I will call the purity of the political, since democracy refers to an aporetic structure of signification that is *always* and *everywhere* the same, even if only "in the West" (this is what we might call the archi-aporia of différance). That it is aporetic, possible only in its impossibility, makes no significant difference: it is as if democracy had a single and unique fundamental form.
149. Angela Y. Davis, *The Angela Y. Davis Reader*, ed. Joy James (Malden, MA: Wiley-Blackwell, 1998), 39.

150. Hobsbawm, *Globalisation, Democracy and Terrorism*, 98–99. He adds: "I am not suggesting that non-democratic regimes are better than democratic regimes. I merely remind you of the fact, which is too often overlooked, that the well-being of countries does not depend on the presence or absence of any single brand of institutional arrangement, however morally commendable" (98–99).

151. See, for example, Amin, *Capitalism in the Age of Globalization*, xxii.

152. We should inquire, in light of this, into the rarefication of political acts in an important strand of contemporary leftist theory. After all, by orchestrating a displacement from a substantialist conception of politics, where doing politics is creating a new state of affairs, to a theorization of politics as rupture, interruption, dissensus, intermittent act, one runs the risk of ultimately rarifying politics, of rendering it entirely exceptional (as is effectively the case in the oligarchies deemed democratic). In order to do this, one is frequently required, moreover, to essentialize politics by purporting to be able to identify what is proper to it. Purified, rarified, essentialized, politics thus suffers a conceptual over-determination that does not take into account the plurality of political actors and conceptions. Politics would apparently only exist when the thinker in question judges that an exceptional act is genuinely deserving of this name. I would refer the reader on this point to my critique of Jacques Rancière's political thought in chapter 6 of Gabriel Rockhill, *Interventions in Contemporary Thought: History, Politics, Aesthetics* (Edinburgh: Edinburgh University Press, 2016).

153. William Blum, *Rogue State: A Guide to the World's Only Superpower*, 3rd ed. (London: Zed Books, 2006), 222–23.

154. On this point, see the perspicacious critique of the logic of "democracy now!" formulated by Samir Amin in "African Economist Samir Amin on the World Social Forum."

155. Bouton, *Taming Democracy*, 107.

156. Cited in Dupuis-Déri, *Démocratie*, 174.

157. Babeuf, *Textes choisis*, 148.

158. Cited in Luciana Canfora, *Democracy in Europe: A History of an Ideology* (Oxford: Blackwell, 2006), 178. For the entire text, see Robespierre, *Pour le bonheur et la liberté : Discours*, ed. Yannick Bosc, Florence Gauthier, and Sophie Wahnich (Paris: La Fabrique éditions, 2000).

159. Parenti, *Democracy for the Few*, 37. See also Chomsky, *Deterring Democracy*, 348.

160. Parenti, *Democracy for the Few*, 38.

161. I am currently working on another project, provisionally entitled *Rethinking, Reworking Revolution*, which might be called more "positive" (to use very schematic language). We should remind ourselves, moreover, especially for the critical reader who only sees here a negative stance, that it is unlikely one would tell a doctor that it is useless to make a diagnosis without knowing in advance the precise cure.

# BIBLIOGRAPHY

Abbate, Janet. *Inventing the Internet.* Cambridge, MA: MIT Press, 1999.
Adams, John. *The Works of John Adams, Second President of the United States: With a Life of the Author, Notes and Illustrations.* Vol. 6. Boston: Charles C. Little and James Brown, 1851.
Agamben, Giorgio, Alain Badiou, Daniel Bensaïd, Wendy Brown, Jean-Luc Nancy, Jacques Rancière, Kristin Ross, and Slavoj Žižek. *Democracy in What State?* Translated by William McCuaig. New York: Columbia University Press, 2009.
Alexander, Michelle. *The New Jim Crow: Mass Incarceration in the Age of Colorblindness.* New York: New Press, 2010.
Amati, Frank, and Tony Aspromourgos. "Petty *contra* Hobbes: A Previously Untranslated Manuscript." *Journal of the History of Ideas* 46, no. 1 (January–March 1985): 127–32.
Amin, Samir. *Capitalism in the Age of Globalization: The Management of Contemporary Society.* London: Zed Books, 2014.
———. *Spectres of Capitalism: A Critique of Current Intellectual Fashions.* New York: Monthly Review Press, 1998.
Amin, Samir, with Amy Goodman and Juan González. "African Economist Samir Amin on the World Social Forum, Globalization and the Barbarism of Capitalism." *Democracy Now!*, March 27, 2015. http://www.democracynow.org/2015/3/27/african_economist_samir_amin_on_the.
Amnesty International. "USA: Below the Radar: Secret Flights to Torture and 'Disappearance.'" April 4, 2006.
Arendt, Hannah. *Between Past and Future.* New York: Penguin, 1968.
Balibar, Étienne. *La philosophie de Marx.* Paris: Éditions La Découverte, 2001.
Bamford, James. "The Spy Factory." PBS, February 3, 2009. http://www.pbs.org/wgbh/nova/spyfactory/program.html.
Barnes, Jonathan. "The Hellenistic Platos." *Apeiron* 24, no. 2 (June 1991): 115–28.
Bauman, Zygmunt. *Globalization: The Human Consequences.* New York: Columbia University Press, 1998.

Bernal, Martin. *Black Athena: The Afroasiatic Roots of Classical Civilization.* Vol. 1: *The Fabrication of Ancient Greece 1785–1985.* New Brunswick, NJ: Rutgers University Press, 1987.

Bienvenu, Richard. *The Ninth of Thermidor: The Fall of Robespierre.* Oxford: Oxford University Press, 1970.

Bilgrami, Akeel. "Democracy and Disenchantment." *Social Scientist* 37, no. 11/12 (November–December 2009): 4–21.

Birch, Anthony H. *The Concepts and Theories of Modern Democracy.* London: Routledge, 1993.

Black, Antony. *A World History of Ancient Political Thought.* Oxford: Oxford University Press, 2009.

Blanqui, Auguste. "'Lettre à Maillard,' June 6, 1852." In *Textes choisis.* Paris: Éditions Sociales, 1971.

Blum, William. *America's Deadliest Export: Democracy and the Truth about US Foreign Policy and Everything Else.* London: Zed Books, 2013.

———. *Rogue State: A Guide to the World's Only Superpower.* 3rd ed. London: Zed Books, 2006.

Bookchin, Murray. *Ecology and Revolutionary Thought.* New York: Times Change Press, 1970.

———. *Post-Scarcity Anarchism.* Palo Alto, CA: Ramparts Press, 1971.

———. *Social Ecology and Communalism.* Oakland, CA: AK Press, 2007.

Bourdieu, Pierre. *Contre-feux.* Paris: Éditions Raisons d'Agir, 1998.

———. *Contre-feux 2: Pour un mouvement social européen.* Paris: Éditions Raisons d'Agir, 2001.

———. *Firing Back: Against the Tyranny of the Market 2.* Translated by Loïc Wacquant. London: Verso, 2003.

Bourdieu, Pierre, and Loïc Wacquant. "NewLiberalSpeak: Notes on the New Planetary Vulgate." Translated by David Macey. *Radical Philosophy* 105 (January–February 2001).

Bouton, Terry. *Taming Democracy: "The People," the Founders, and the Troubled Ending of the American Revolution.* Oxford: Oxford University Press, 2007.

Cahall, Bailey, David Sterman, Emily Schneider, and Peter Bergen. "Do NSA's Bulk Surveillance Programs Stop Terrorists?" Policy Paper, January 13, 2014. www.newamerica.net/publications/policy/do_nsas_bulk_surveillance_programs_stop_terrorists.

Canfora, Luciana. *Democracy in Europe: A History of an Ideology.* Oxford: Blackwell, 2006.

Castoriadis, Cornelius. *The Castoriadis Reader.* Translated by David A. Curtis. Oxford: Blackwell, 1997.

———. *Crossroads in the Labyrinth.* Translated by Kate Soper and Martin H. Ryle. Cambridge, MA: MIT Press, 1984.

———. *Figures of the Thinkable.* Translated by Helen Arnold. Stanford, CA: Stanford University Press, 2007.

———. *The Imaginary Institution of Society*. Translated by Kathleen Blamey. Cambridge, MA: MIT Press, 1987.
———. *Le monde morcelé: Les carrefours du labyrinth 3*. Paris: Éditions du Seuil, 1990.
———. *La montée de l'insignifiance*. Paris: Éditions du Seuil, 1996.
———. *Postscript on Insignificance: Dialogues with Cornelius Castoriadis*. Edited by Gabriel Rockhill. Translated by Gabriel Rockhill and John V. Garner. London: Continuum, 2011.
Chaplin, Charlie. *My Autobiography*. New York: Simon and Schuster, 1964.
Chardel, Pierre-Antoine, and Gabriel Rockhill, eds. *Technologies de contrôle dans la mondialisation: Enjeux politiques, éthiques et esthétiques*. Paris: Éditions Kimé, 2009.
Chatterjee, Partha. *Lineages of Political Society*. New York: Columbia University Press, 2011.
———. *The Politics of the Governed: Reflections on Popular Politics in Most of the World*. New York: Columbia University Press, 2004.
Choma, Russ. "Millionaires' Club: For First Time, Most Lawmakers Are Worth $1 Million-Plus." *OpenSecrets Blog*, January 9, 2014. http://www.opensecrets.org/news/2014/01/millionaires-club-for-first-time-most-lawmakers-are-worth-1-million-plus.html.
Chomsky, Noam. *The Chomsky Trilogy*. Tucson: Odonian, 1997.
———. *Deterring Democracy*. New York: Hill and Wang, 1991.
Christensen, Christian. "Wikileaks et les mythes de l'ère numérique." *Le monde diplomatique* 678 (September 2010).
Clarke, Richard. *Against All Enemies: Inside America's War on Terror*. New York: Free Press, 2004.
"Clinton Signs Legislation Overhauling Bank Laws." *New York Times*, November 13, 1999.
Congressional Research Service Report for Congress. "Renditions: Constraints Imposed by Laws on Torture." October 12, 2007.
Cordellier, Serge, ed. *La mondialisation au-delà des mythes*. Paris: La Découverte, 1997.
Council of Europe. "Allégations de détentions secrètes et de transferts interétatiques illégaux de détenus concernant des Etats membres du Conseil de l'Europe." June 12, 2006.
———. "Détentions secrètes et transferts illégaux de détenus impliquant des Etats membres du Conseil de l'Europe." June 11, 2007.
Curran, James, Natalie Fenton, and Des Freedman. *Misunderstanding the Internet*. New York: Routledge, 2012.
Dagorn, René. "Une brève histoire du mot 'mondialisation.'" In *Mondialisation: Les mots et les choses*, edited by GEMDEV. Paris: Éditions Karthala, 1999.
Dahl, Robert A. *On Democracy*. New Haven, CT: Yale University Press, 2000.
Dallmayr, Fred. "Liberal Democracy and Its Critics: Some Voices from East and West." In *Democratic Culture: Historical and Philosophical Essays*, edited by Akeel Bilgrami, 1–22. New York: Routledge, 2011.

Davis, Angela Y. *The Angela Y. Davis Reader*. Edited by Joy James. Malden, MA: Wiley-Blackwell, 1998.

Davis, Mike. "Planet of Slums." *New Left Review* 26 (March–April 2004).

Deleuze, Gilles. *Negotiations: 1972–1990*. Translated by Martin Joughin. New York: Columbia University Press, 1995.

Deraismes, Maria. *Ce que veulent les femmes: Articles et conférences de 1869 à 1891*. Paris: Éditions Syros, 1980.

Derrida, Jacques. *Rogues: Two Essays on Reason*. Translated by Pascale-Anne Brault and Michael Naas. Stanford, CA: Stanford University Press, 2005.

———. *Specters of Marx: The State of the Debt, the Work of Mourning and the New International*. Translated by Peggy Kamuf. New York: Routledge, 2006.

Douglass, Frederick. *Selected Speeches and Writings*. Edited by Philip S. Foner. Chicago: Lawrence Hill, 1999.

Dupuis-Déri, Francis. *Démocratie: Histoire politique d'un mot aux États-Unis et en France*. Montréal: Lux Éditeur, 2013.

Fanon, Frantz. *Toward the African Revolution: Political Essays*. Translated by Haakon Chevalier. New York: Grove, 1967.

Farrand, Max, ed. *The Records of the Federal Convention of 1787*. Vol. 1. New Haven, CT: Yale University Press, 1987.

Fassin, Didier. *L'ombre du monde: Une anthropologie de la condition carcérale*. Paris: Éditions du Seuil, 2015.

Feenberg, Andrew. *Transforming Technology: A Critical Theory Revisited*. Oxford: Oxford University Press, 2002.

Finley, Moses I. *Ancient Slavery and Modern Ideology*. Princeton, NJ: Markus Wiener, 1998.

———. *Democracy Ancient and Modern*. New Brunswick, NJ: Rutgers University Press, 1985.

———. *Politics in the Ancient World*. Cambridge: Cambridge University Press, 1983.

Flusser, Vilém. *Towards a Philosophy of Photography*. London: Reaktion Books, 2000.

Friedman, Milton. *Capitalism and Freedom*. Chicago: University of Chicago Press, 1982.

Fromm, Erich. *The Sane Society*. New York: Routledge, 1956.

Fukuyama, Francis. *The End of History and the Last Man*. New York: Avon Books, 1992.

———. "The End of History Revisited." Lecture presented to the Long Now Foundation, San Francisco, June 28, 2007. http://fora.tv/2007/06/28/Francis_Fukuyama_End_Of_History_Revisited#%20.

Giddens, Anthony. *The Consequences of Modernity*. Stanford, CA: Stanford University Press, 1990.

Gilens, Martin. "Scholar behind Viral 'Oligarchy' Study Tells You What It Means." *Talking Points Memo*, April 22, 2014. http://talkingpointsmemo.com/dc/princeton-scholar-demise-of-democracy-america-tpm-interview.

Gilens, Martin, and Benjamin I. Page. "Testing Theories of American Politics: Elites, Interest Groups, and Average Citizens." *Perspectives on Politics* 12, no. 3 (September 2014): 564–81.
Gitelman, Lisa. *Always Already New: Media, History, and the Data of Culture.* Cambridge, MA: MIT Press, 2006.
Goody, Jack. *The Theft of History.* Cambridge: Cambridge University Press, 2007.
Graeber, David. *The Democracy Project: A History, a Crisis, a Movement.* London: Allen Lane, 2012.
———. *Possibilities: Essays on Hierarchy, Rebellion, and Desire.* Oakland, CA: AK Press, 2007.
Grandin, Greg. *Empire's Workshop: Latin America, the United States, and the Rise of the New Imperialism.* New York: Metropolitan Books, 2010.
Graubard, Stephen R. "Democracy." In *Dictionary of the History of Ideas*, edited by Philip P. Wiener, 652–67. New York: Charles Scribner's Sons, 1973.
Greenwald, Glenn, with Juan González. "Growing Backlash against NSA Spying Shows Why U.S. Wants to Silence Edward Snowden." *Democracy Now!*, July 18, 2013. http://www.democracynow.org/2013/7/18/glenn_greenwald_growing _backlash_against_nsa.
"A Guide to the Memos on Torture." *New York Times.* http://www.nytimes.com/ref /international/24MEMO-GUIDE.html (accessed January 1, 2016).
Harvey, David. *A Brief History of Neoliberalism.* Oxford: Oxford University Press, 2005.
———. *Spaces of Global Capitalism: Towards a Theory of Uneven Geographical Development.* London: Verso, 2006.
Havelock, Eric Alfred. "The Evidence for the Teaching Socrates." *Transactions and Proceedings of the American Philological Association* 65 (1934): 282–95.
———. *Preface to Plato.* Cambridge, MA: Belknap Press of Harvard University Press, 1963.
Held, David, and Anthony McGrew, eds. *The Global Transformations Reader.* Cambridge: Polity, 2003.
Held, David, Anthony McGrew, David Goldblatt, and Jonathan Perraton. *Global Transformations: Politics, Economics and Culture.* Stanford, CA: Stanford University Press, 1999.
Herder, J. G. *Philosophical Writings.* Edited and translated by Michael N. Forster. Cambridge: Cambridge University Press, 2002.
Hirst, Paul, and Grahame Thompson, eds. *Globalization in Question.* Cambridge: Polity, 1999.
Hobsbawm, Eric. *Globalization, Democracy and Terrorism.* London: Abacus, 2007.
Hudson, Michael. "Obama's Awful Financial Recovery Plan." *CounterPunch*, February 12, 2009.
Human Rights Watch. 2014 World Report. http://www.hrw.org/world-report /2014.

Hume, David. *Selected Essays*. Edited by Steven Copley and Andrew Edgar. Oxford: Oxford University Press, 1998.

Hyest, Jean-Jacques, and Guy-Pierre Cabanel. "Les conditions de détention dans les établissements pénitentiaires en France." June 29, 2000. http://www.senat.fr/rap/199-449/199-449.html.

Isakhan, Benjamin, and Stephen Stockwell, eds. *The Secret History of Democracy*. New York: Palgrave Macmillan, 2011.

Israel, Jonathan. "The Intellectual Origins of Modern Democratic Republicanism (1660–1720)." *European Journal of Political Theory* 3, no. 7 (2004): 7–36.

———. *Radical Enlightenment*. Oxford: Oxford University Press, 2001.

Johnson, Chalmers. "We Have the Bailout Money—We're Spending It on War." *The Nation*, September 29, 2008.

Kant, Immanuel. *Toward Perpetual Peace and Other Writings on Politics, Peace, and History*. Translated by David L. Colclasure. New Haven, CT: Yale University Press, 2006.

Ketcham, Ralph Louis, ed. *The Anti-Federalist Papers and the Constitutional Convention Debates*. New York: Signet, 2003.

King, Martin Luther, Jr. *A Testament of Hope: The Essential Writings and Speeches of Martin Luther King, Jr.* New York: HarperCollins, 1986.

Klein, Naomi. Lecture at the University of Chicago, October 6, 2008. http://www.democracynow.org/2008/10/6/naomi_klein.

———. *The Shock Doctrine: The Rise of Disaster Capitalism*. New York: Picador, 2008.

Koelble, Thomas A., and Edward Lipuma. "Democratizing Democracy: A Postcolonial Critique of Conventional Approaches to the 'Measurement of Democracy.'" *Democratization* 15, no. 1 (2008): 1–28.

Kuhn, Thomas. *The Essential Tension*. Chicago: University of Chicago Press, 1977.

Kymlicka, Will. "The New Debate on Minority Rights (and Postscript)." In *Multiculturalism and Political Theory*, edited by Anthony Simon Laden and David Owen. Cambridge: Cambridge University Press, 2007.

Laclau, Ernesto, and Chantal Mouffe. *Hegemony and Socialist Strategy*. London: Verso, 2001.

Laniel, Bertlinde. *Le mot "democracy" et son histoire aux États-Unis de 1780 à 1856*. Saint-Étienne: Publications de l'Université de Saint-Étienne, 1995.

Lebaron, Frédéric. *Le savant, le politique et la mondialisation*. Bellecombe-en-Bauges: Éditions du Croquant, 2003.

Lee, Chisun. "Bush's Secret Counterterrorism Law Book—and the Demands to Release It." *ProPublica*, January 28, 2009. http://www.propublica.org/article/obama-inherits-bushs-secret-counterterrorism-law-book-and-the-demands-to-re.

Lenin, V. I. *The State and Revolution*. Chicago: Haymarket Books, 2014.

Lévêque, Pierre, and Pierre Vidal-Naquet. *Cleisthenes the Athenian: An Essay on the Representation of Space and Time in Greek Political Thought from the End of the Sixth Century to the Death of Plato*. Translated by David A. Curtis. New York: Prometheus, 1996.

Lévy, Edmond. *La Grèce au Ve siècle: de Clisthène à Socrate*. Paris: Éditions du Seuil, 1997.

Locke, John. *Locke: Political Essays*. Edited by Mark Goldie. Cambridge: Cambridge University Press, 1997.

———. *Two Treatises of Government*. Cambridge: Cambridge University Press, 1988.

Macherey, Pierre. *Le Sujet des norms*. Paris: Éditions Amsterdam, 2014.

Marcuse, Herbert. *An Essay on Liberation*. Boston: Beacon, 1969.

Martin, Marcel, ed. *Charles Chaplin*. Paris: Éditions Seghers, 1972.

Marx, Karl. *Critique of Hegel's "Philosophy of Right."* 1843; Cambridge: Cambridge University Press, 1982.

———. *The Eighteenth Brumaire of Louis Bonaparte*. New York: International Publishers, 1963.

———. "A Letter on Russia." *New International* 1, no. 4 (November 1934).

Mill, John Stuart. *Considerations on Representative Government*. 1861; Cambridge: Cambridge University Press, 2010.

Monnier, Raymonde. "Démocratie et Révolution française." *Mots* 59 (1999).

Montesquieu. *The Spirit of the Laws*. Translated and edited by Anne M. Cohler, Basia Carolyn Miller, and Harold Samuel Stone. Cambridge: Cambridge University Press, 1989.

Munck, Ronaldo. "Neoliberalism, Necessitarianism and Alternatives in Latin America: There Is No Alternative (TINA)?" *Third World Quarterly* 24, no. 3 (June 2003): 495–511.

Neihardt, John G. *Black Elk Speaks: The Complete Edition*. Lincoln: University of Nebraska Press, 2014.

Nichols, John, and Robert Waterman McChesney. *Dollarocracy: How the Money and Media Election Complex Is Destroying America*. New York: Nation Books, 2013.

"Only 30% of Americans Trust Our Government." *Infowars*, March 12, 2013. http://www.infowars.com/only-30-of-americans-trust-our-government/.

Oxfam. "An Economy for the 1%." January 19, 2016. https://www.oxfam.org/sites/www.oxfam.org/files/file_attachments/bp210-economy-one-percent-tax-havens-180116-en_0.pdf.

Padis, Marc-Olivier. "Introduction: Entre néolibéralisme et régulation. L'État à la croisée des chemins." *Esprit* 349 (November 2008).

Paine, Thomas. *Rights of Man*. New York: Dover, 1999.

Palmer, R. R. *The Age of Democratic Revolution: A Political History of Europe and America 1760–1800*. Princeton, NJ: Princeton University Press, 2014.

———. "Notes on the Use of the Word 'Democracy' 1789–1799." *Political Science Quarterly* 68, no. 2 (June 1953): 203–26.

Parenti, Michael. *Democracy for the Few*. 8th ed. Boston: Thomson Wadsworth, 2008.

Parry, Geraint. *Political Elites*. London: George Allen and Unwin, 1969.

Perkins, John. *Confessions of an Economic Hit Man.* New York: Plume, 2006.
Plenel, Edwy. "Nous sommes tous de WikiLeaks!" *Mediapart*, December 22, 2010.
Pleyers, Geoffrey. *Alter-Globalization: Becoming Actors in the Global Age.* Cambridge: Polity, 2010.
Polanyi, Karl. *The Great Transformation.* Boston: Beacon, 1944.
———. *The Great Transformation: The Political and Economic Origins of Our Time.* Boston: Beacon, 2001.
Priest, Dana. "Wrongful Imprisonment: Anatomy of a CIA Mistake." *Washington Post*, December 4, 2005.
Rancière, Jacques. *La haine de la démocratie.* Paris: Éditions La Fabrique, 2006.
———. *Hatred of Democracy.* New York: Verso, 2009.
———. *The Politics of Aesthetics: The Distribution of the Sensible.* Edited and translated by Gabriel Rockhill. New York: Continuum, 2004.
Reilly, Mollie. "Obama Told Aides He's 'Really Good at Killing People,' New Book 'Double Down' Claims." *Huffington Post*, November 3, 2013. http://www.huffingtonpost.com/2013/11/03/obamadrones-double-down_n_4208815.html.
Rimbaud, Arthur. *Collected Poems.* Oxford: Oxford University Press, 2001.
———. *Œuvres complètes.* Edited by Antoine Adam. Paris: Éditions Gallimard, 1972.
Rivière, Philippe. "WikiLeaks, mort au messager." *Le monde diplomatique*, January 2011.
Robertson, Ewan. "Former US President Carter: Venezuelan Electoral System 'Best in the World.'" *venezuelanalysis.com*, September 22, 2012. http://venezuelanalysis.com/news/7272.
Robertson, Roland. *Globalization: Social Theory and Global Culture.* London: Sage, 1992.
Robespierre, Maximilien. *Pour le bonheur et la liberté: Discours.* Edited by Yannick Bosc, Florence Gauthier, and Sophie Wahnich. Paris: La Fabrique éditions, 2000.
Rockhill, Gabriel. "La démocratie dans l'histoire des cultures politiques." In *Jacques Rancière ou la politique à l'œuvre*, edited by Jérôme Game and Aliocha Lasowski, 55–71. Paris: Éditions Archives Contemporaines, series "Centre d'Études Poétiques," 2009.
———. *Interventions in Contemporary Thought: History, Politics, Aesthetics.* Edinburgh: Edinburgh University Press, 2016.
———. *Logique de l'histoire: Pour une analytique des pratiques philosophiques.* Paris: Éditions Hermann, 2010.
Romilly, Jacqueline de. *Problèmes de la démocratie grecque.* Paris: Éditions Hermann, 1975.
Rosanvallon, Pierre. "The History of the Word 'Democracy' in France." Translated by Philip J. Costopoulous. *Journal of Democracy* 6, no. 4 (October 1995): 140–54.
Rosenberg, Justin. *The Follies of Globalisation Theory.* London: Verso, 2002.
Rossiter, Clinton, ed. *The Federalist Papers: Alexander Hamilton, James Madison, John Jay.* New York: Signet Classic, 2003.

Rousseau, Jean-Jacques. *Basic Political Writings.* Translated and edited by Donald A. Cress. Indianapolis: Hackett, 1987.

———. *Discours sur l'origine et les fondements de l'inégalité parmi les hommes / Discours sur les sciences et les arts.* Paris: Garnier-Flammarion, 1992.

Sanders, Richard. "GATS: The End of Democracy?" *Australian Financial Review,* June 15, 2001. http://australiatoday.webs.com/documents/GATS_End_of_Democracy_Sanders01.pdf.

Sartre, Jean-Paul. *Critique de la raison dialectique.* Vol. 1. Paris: Éditions Gallimard, 1960.

———. *La responsabilité de l'écrivain.* Paris: Éditions Verdier, 1998.

Saxonhouse, Arlene W. "Athenian Democracy: Modern Mythmakers and Ancient Theorists." *PS: Political Science and Politics* 26, no. 3 (September 1993): 486–90.

Scahill, Jeremy. *Blackwater: The Rise of the World's Most Powerful Mercenary Army.* New York: Nation Books, 2008.

Sen, Amartya. "Democracy and Its Global Roots." *New Republic,* October 6, 2003, 28–35.

———. "Democracy as a Universal Value." *Journal of Democracy* 10, no. 3 (1999): 3–17.

Sharp, Andrew, ed. *The English Levellers.* Cambridge: Cambridge University Press, 1998.

*Social Imaginaries* 1, no. 1 (2015).

Soueif, Ahdaf. "Amidst Egypt's Bloodshed, 'We Are Trying to Keep the Discourse of the Revolution Alive.'" *Democracy Now!,* August 19, 2013. http://www.democracynow.org/2013/8/19/ahdaf_soueif_amidst_egypts_bloodshed_we.

Spinoza, Baruch. *Theological-Political Treatise.* Cambridge: Cambridge University Press, 2007.

Stelter, Brian. "NBC Wins Battle over Debate." *New York Times,* January 15, 2008. http://thecaucus.blogs.nytimes.com/2008/01/15/nbc-wins-battle-overdebate/?_php=true&_type=blogs&_r=0.

Stiegler, Bernard. *Philosopher par accident: Entretiens avec Elie During.* Paris: Éditions Galilée, 2004.

Stiglitz, Joseph. *Globalization and Its Discontents.* New York: W. W. Norton, 2002.

Storing, Herbert J., ed. *The Complete Anti-Federalist.* Vol. 2. Chicago: University of Chicago Press, 2008.

Swindler, William F., ed. *Sources and Documents of United States Constitutions.* Vol. 8. Dobbs Ferry, NY: Oceana, 1979.

Taibbi, Matt, with Amy Goodman and Aaron Maté. "Who Goes to Jail?" *Democracy Now!,* April 15, 2014. http://www.democracynow.org/2014/4/15/who_goes_to_jail_matt_taibbi.

Tocqueville, Alexis de. *Democracy in America.* Translated by Henry Reeve. Washington, DC: Regnery, 2002.

United Nations. *The Challenge of the Slums.* New York: United Nations, 2003.

Vico, Giambattista. *New Science.* Translated by Dave Marsh. London: Penguin, 1999.

Vidal-Naquet, Pierre. *Le chasseur noir: Formes de pensée et formes de société dans le monde grec.* Paris: Éditions La Découverte, 2005.

Vile, John R., ed. *The Constitutional Convention of 1787: A Comprehensive Encyclopedia of America's Founding.* Santa Barbara, CA: ABC-CLIO, 2005.

Wallach, John R. "None of Us Is a Democrat Now." *Theory and Event* 13, no. 2 (2010).

Wallerstein, Immanuel. "After Developmentalism and Globalization, What?" *Social Forces* 83, no. 3 (March 2005): 1263–78.

———. *World-Systems Analysis: An Introduction.* Durham, NC: Duke University Press, 2004.

Whitman, Walt. *Democratic Vistas and Other Papers.* Amsterdam: Fredonia Books, 2002.

———. *The Works of Walt Whitman.* Ware, England: Wordsworth, 1995.

Williams, Raymond. *Culture and Society 1780–1950.* London: Penguin, 1961.

———. *Television: Technology and Cultural Form.* New York: Routledge, 2003.

Wing, Nick. "Jimmy Carter Defends Edward Snowden, Says NSA Spying Has Compromised Nation's Democracy." *Huffington Post*, July 18, 2013. http://www.huffingtonpost.com/2013/07/18/jimmy-carter-edward-snowden_n_3616930.html.

Witness. "Outlawed: Extraordinary Rendition, Torture and Disappearances in the 'War on Terror.'" http://hub.witness.org/en/Outlawed (accessed January 1, 2016).

Wolf, Martin. "Keynes Offers Us the Best Way to Think about the Financial Crisis." *Financial Times*, December 23, 2008. http://www.ft.com/intl/cms/s/0/be2dbf2c-d113-11dd-8cc3-000077b07658.html#axzz3w8TtuFiG.

Wolf, Naomi. "The Shocking Truth about the Crackdown on Occupy." *Guardian*, November 25, 2011. http://www.theguardian.com/commentisfree/cifamerica/2011/nov/25/shocking-truth-about-crackdown-occupy.

Wolin, Sheldon. *Democracy Incorporated: Managed Democracy and the Specter of Inverted Totalitarianism.* Princeton, NJ: Princeton University Press, 2010.

Wootton, David. "Leveller Democracy and the Puritan Revolution." In *The Cambridge History of Political Thought 1450–1700*, edited by J. H. Burns with Mark Goldie. Cambridge: Cambridge University Press, 2014.

Zinn, Howard. *A People's History of the United States.* New York: Harper, 2015.

# INDEX

Abbate, Janet, 39
Abu Ghraib prison scandal, 36, 83
Adams, John, 71, 127n108
Alexander, Michelle, 83
Algeria, 63
Althusser, Louis, 112n21
Amerindians, 52, 72, 84, 97, 125n76
Anderson, Perry, 5
"apriorism, essentialist," 30
Arendt, Hannah, 115n51
Aristotle, 65
Assange, Julian, 83, 91
*Aufhebung*, 17

Babeuf, Gracchus, 73, 100
Badiou, Alain, 78
Balibar, Étienne, 79, 115n45
Barnave, Antoine, 74
Barnes, Jonathan, 44
Bauman, Zygmunt, 113n26
Benjamin, Walter, 40, 41
Bensaïd, Daniel, 56, 94
Berlusconi, Silvio, 79, 98
Bill of Rights, 84–86, 90–92. *See also* U.S. Constitution
Birch, Anthony H., 65
Black Elk, 52
Blanqui, Auguste, 74
Bloch, Joseph, 28
Blum, William, 81–82, 99
Bookchin, Murray, 41, 117n22

Bourdieu, Pierre, 115n46, 116n60
Brown, Wendy, 78, 79, 94
Bush, George W., 22, 79, 98

Camus, Albert, 103
capitalism, 16, 24, 29; democracy and, 17, 20, 55, 97, 100–101; no alternative to, 16, 18, 22, 32, 55; post-Fordist, 13. *See also* neoliberalism
Carter, Jimmy, 85, 89
Castoriadis, Cornelius, 21, 29–30, 112n21; on democracy, 87, 90, 93; on election system, 89; on public opinion, 45, 129n128, 131n145; on technological progress, 38–39, 42, 44–45
Chaplin, Charlie, 46–48, 118n31
Chatterjee, Partha, 63, 126n94
Chomsky, Noam, 81, 82
Christensen, Christian, 118n35
Citizens United, 90
*City Lights* (film), 47
climate change, 110n6
Clinton, Hillary, 91
Cobbett, William, 71
Colombia, 98
colonial historiography, 2, 56, 63
commonwealth, 67
communism. *See* Marxism
conjuncture, 2–9, 15, 19, 22, 27–28, 101, 103, 104; democracy and, 58, 62–65, 78–82, 87, 93, 101–4; technology and, 38, 42, 48

constitution: Carolina, 67, 100; Rhode Island, 68. *See also* U.S. Constitution
control societies, 35–36
counter-education, 93–94
counter-history of the present, 3–4, 8–11, 103–7; democracy and, 54–55, 59; globalization and, 21–22, 27, 31–32; technology and, 38
Curran, James, 39–40

Dahl, Robert A., 60, 78
Davis, Angela, 97
Declaration of the Rights of Man and of the Citizen, 100
de la Court, Johan, 68
Deleuze, Gilles, 35–36, 79
democracy, 2, 4, 30, 51–102, 105–6; actually existing, 9, 53, 58, 79–97, 101, 104; Athenian, 55–56, 64–66, 70, 121n17, 121n20; Babeuf on, 73; Badiou on, 78; Blum on , 99; capitalism and, 17, 20, 55, 97, 100–101; Castoriadis on, 87, 90, 93; Chomsky on, 82; commonwealth versus, 67; Dahl on, 60; Deleuze on, 79; Derrida on, 131n148; early modern, 66–68; Enlightenment thinkers on, 68–70; Fanon on, 63; Fukuyama on, 57–58; historical imaginary of, 54, 61–62, 80; Hobsbawm on, 78, 79, 98, 132n150; intransitive history of, 60–79, 96–97; Kant on, 70, 131n148; Laniel on, 68, 73, 78, 125n72; Lenin on, 77; Locke on, 67; Marcuse on, 77, 79–80; Montesquieu on, 69; Orwell on, 51; Parenti on, 100–101; performative contradictions of, 79–95; phases of, 60–79; political imaginary of, 51, 53–54, 61–62, 94, 101; postcolonial, 63; as problematic term, 52, 60–61, 78–79, 88, 101; radical, 77; Rancière on, 78, 112n23; republicanism versus, 70–71, 87–88, 123n53, 127n108; Rimbaud on, 56, 75, 76, 120n8; Robespierre on, 73; Rosanvallon on, 66, 74, 78, 79, 123n43,
124n62; Rousseau on, 68–70, 87, 99; rule of law and, 84–85, 94; Sartre on, 57, 78; Spinoza on, 68; Swiss, 66–67; theodicy and, 57–60, 101; Thoreau on, 95; Tocqueville on, 57, 74; value-concept of, 8, 51–57, 94, 101; Vico on, 70; Whitman on, 75–76
"democratophilia," 55, 73–79, 131n148
Deng Xiaoping, 16
Deraismes, Maria, 119n4
Derrida, Jacques, 43, 79, 131n148
determinism: economic, 6, 17–19, 24, 29, 105, 112n22, 116n59; historical, 6, 8, 9, 28–30, 115n51; technological, 6, 17–19, 29, 40–42, 45, 105
DeWitt, John, 72
"dollarocracy," 91
Douglass, Frederick, 119n3
Dupuis-Déri, Francis, 73, 124n66

ecology, 24, 110n6; technological, 28, 34, 41–42, 49, 117n22
economic determinism, 6, 17–19, 24, 29, 105, 112n22, 116n59
Edison, Thomas, 45–46
elections, 79, 90–94, 99; Castoriadis on, 89; Fromm on, 90; Parenti on, 129n131; Rousseau on, 87, 99; voter turnout for, 89, 92. *See also* voting rights
emancipation, 48, 72
"end of history," 8, 19, 30, 51, 57, 60–62
Engels, Friedrich, 28
epochal thinking, 3, 7, 34–38, 45, 48, 103–4
essentialism: historical, 37; technological, 40–45
"essentialist apriorism," 30

Fanon, Frantz, 63
Fassin, Didier, 117n8
Feenberg, Andrew, 45
Fenton, Natalie, 40
financial crisis of 2008, 22–23, 31
Findley, William, 100

Finley, Moses, 66
First World War, 81
Flusser, Vilém, 116n3
Foucault, Michel, 35
Freedman, Des, 40
freedom, 6, 16, 18; Kant on, 70; Rousseau on, 87, 99; Spinoza on, 68; Valéry on, 51. *See also* Bill of Rights
Friedman, Milton, 16
Fromm, Erich, 90
Fukuyama, Francis, 8, 19, 51, 57–58, 112n22

Gaumont films, 46
gender issues, 66, 72, 84–85, 97, 119n4, 125n82
Gerry, Elbridge, 72
Giddens, Anthony, 24–25, 114n43
Gilens, Martin, 91
Gitelman, Lisa, 110n5
globalization, 4–7, 11–32; Bauman on, 113n26; Bourdieu on, 115n46, 116n60; Giddens on, 114n43; Gitelman on, 110n5; Hobsbawm on, 12; ideology of, 21–27, 105–6, 112n18; political imaginary of, 27–28, 31–32. *See also* neoliberalism
global warming, 110n6
Goldblatt, David, 24
Goldman Sachs, 22–23
Graeber, David, 62, 73, 121n16
*Great Dictator, The* (film), 47–48
Greenwald, Glenn, 85
Guantánamo prison, 36, 83

Hamas, 98
Hamilton, Alexander, 71, 72, 123n53, 127n108
Harvey, David, 22
Havelock, Eric, 44
Hayek, Friedrich, 22
Hegel, G. W. F., 19, 56, 57, 112n22
Held, David, 23–24, 26
Henry, Patrick, 72
Herder, Johann Gottfried von, 13–14

historical determinism, 6, 8, 9, 28–30, 115n51
historical imaginary, 3, 5, 103–5; definition of, 109n1; of democracy, 54, 61–62, 80; epochal thinking of, 3; of Marxism, 20–21
historical metastasis, 4, 39, 61, 65, 76
historical methodology, 4, 37, 44, 87
historical order, 3–7, 19, 23–24, 35, 59, 101; of political imaginary, 9, 28, 31–32, 80, 104–6. *See also* history, logic of
historicism: radical, 8, 28, 53–54, 61; reductive, 8, 17–18, 45
historiography, 31; colonial, 2, 56, 63; Marxist, 5–6, 18, 32; ontogenetic, 62; Whig, 59, 84–85, 93–94
history: dimensions of, 3–7, 13, 34–37, 48, 59–61, 76–77, 103–4; "end" of, 8, 19, 30, 51, 57, 60–62; of future, 13, 32, 105–7; logic of, 4, 8, 19–20, 39, 44, 59, 80. *See also* counter-history of the present; historical order
Hitler, Adolf, 98
Hobbes, Thomas, 122n31
Hobsbawm, Eric, 12; on democracy, 78, 79, 98, 132n150
human rights, 36, 78
Hume, David, 70
"hyperglobalizers," 24–25, 111n10

*idée-force*, 6, 21, 25, 32, 112n23
ideology, 36–37; globalization as, 21–27, 105–6, 112n18; political imaginary and, 21, 26–28, 109n1
imaginary. *See* historical imaginary; political imaginary
information and communication technologies (ICT), 33
information technologies, 33
"internationalization," 16
International Monetary Fund (IMF), 12
International Telecommunication Union, 37

Internet access, 2, 12, 37–40
intransitive history, of democracy, 60–79, 96–97
Isakhan, Benjamin, 63, 121n20
isonomy, 66, 94
Israel, Jonathan, 68

Jackson, Andrew, 73
Japanese Americans, 85

Kant, Immanuel, 70, 131n148
Ketcham, Ralph, 70–71
Keynes, John Maynard, 22
Klein, Naomi, 22, 127n102
Kucinich, Dennis, 129n128
Kuhn, Thomas, 14, 27

Laclau, Ernesto, 30
laissez-faire economics, 23, 30–31, 116n58; "freedom" of, 6, 16, 18
Laniel, Bertlinde, 68, 73, 78, 125n72
Lebaron, Frédéric, 15
Lehman Brothers' bankruptcy, 22
Lenin, Vladimir, 77
Levellers, 67
liberalism, 5, 17, 21, 66, 77–78; Bill of Rights and, 84–85; Fukuyama on, 57, 112n22; political equality under, 84–85; Polyani on, 30–31, 76–77, 126n83; Whig history of, 84, 93–94. *See also* neoliberalism
logic of history. *See* history, logic of; historical order
Locke, John, 67
Lyotard, Jean-François, 5, 38

Macherey, Pierre, 109n1
Madison, James, 71
Mann, Michael, 112n18
Manning, Chelsea, 83
Marcuse, Herbert, 77, 79–80, 115n49, 131n147
Marx, Karl, 19, 57, 112n22; on Russia, 28–29

Marxism, 17–21, 23, 77–78; historical determinism of, 29–30; historical imaginary of, 20–21; historiography of, 5–6, 32; realizability of, 58–59, 112n21
Mason, George, 72
McChesney, Robert, 91
*McCutcheon v. FEC*, 90–91
McGrew, Anthony, 23–24, 26
metanarratives, 5, 38, 56, 102
metastasis, historical, 4, 39, 61, 65, 76
Military Commissions Act, 23, 83
Mises, Ludwig von, 22
Montesquieu, 68–69
Mouffe, Chantal, 30
movies, talking, 45–48, 118n31

National Security Agency (NSA), 83, 85–86
Nazi Germany, 98
neoliberalism, 5–6, 16–23, 56, 97; as ideology, 23–25, 27, 105–6, 112n18; as metanarrative, 5, 38, 102; political imaginary and, 27–28, 31–32, 115n46. *See also* globalization
New American Foundation, 86
Nichols, Michael, 91
Nietzsche, Friedrich, 1
normative blackmail, 21, 32, 52, 80, 101, 105
North Carolina constitution, 100

Obama, Barack, 91, 114n35, 127n107, 129n128
Occupy movement, 86, 128n115
Orwell, George, 51
Oxfam organization, 109n2

Page, Benjamin I., 91
*paideia*, 66, 93
Paine, Thomas, 73
Palestine, 98
Palmer, R. R., 78, 79
Parenti, Michael, 85, 92, 100–101, 126n100, 129n131
Paris Commune (1871), 75

146 | INDEX

Patriot Act, 23, 82, 85
Paulson, Henry, 22
Pennsylvania, 100
Perkins, John, 116n55
Perraton, Jonathan, 24
Petty, William, 122n36
phase, definition of, 4, 61
Pinochet, Augusto, 16
Plato, 42–44, 116n1, 131n148
Polanyi, Karl, 22, 23, 30–31, 76–77, 126n83
political imaginary, 1, 2, 8, 9; Bourdieu on, 115n46; capitalism and, 16; democracy and, 51, 53–54, 61–62, 94, 101; globalization and, 27–28, 31–32; historical order of, 9, 28, 31–32, 80, 104–6; ideology and, 21–23, 26–28, 109n1
postmodernism, 4, 5, 24–25, 33–38
praxi-concept, 17, 80
prisons, 23, 36, 83, 85
progress: as metanarrative, 5, 38, 102; technological, 38–39, 42, 44–45; teleological, 17, 18, 59
public opinion, 45, 90, 129n1
public sphere, 90
"purification of the political," 9, 55, 95–102, 131n148, 132n152

racism, 83–85, 97
radical democracy, 77
radical historicism, 8, 28, 53–54, 61
Rancière, Jacques, 40–41, 78, 112n23
Randolph, Edmund, 71–72
Rasmussen Reports, 92
Reagan, Ronald, 16, 79
rendition, extraordinary, 23, 83
republicanism, 70–71, 87–88, 123n53, 127n108
Rhode Island constitution, 68
Rimbaud, Arthur, 56, 75, 76, 120n8
Robespierre, Maximilien de, 73, 100
Rosanvallon, Pierre, 66, 74, 78, 79, 123n43, 124n62
Ross, Kristin, 74–75, 88
Rouch, Jean, 28

Rousseau, Jean-Jacques, 13–14; on democracy, 68–70, 87, 99
rule of law, 84–85, 94
Russia, 28–29

Sanders, Richard, 20–21
Sartre, Jean-Paul, 57, 78
Scott-Heron, Gil, 79
Second World War, 81, 82, 85
Sen, Amartya, 63
sexism, 66, 72, 84–85, 97, 125n82
Sherman, Robert, 72
Sieyès, Abbé, 74
silent movies, 45–48, 118n31
Snowden, Edward, 83, 85, 119n35
South Carolina constitution, 67
Spinoza, Baruch, 68
Stiegler, Bernard, 33, 42–44, 116n1
Stiglitz, Joseph, 6–7
Stockwell, Stephen, 63
Swiss democracy, 66–67

Taibbi, Matt, 128n115
talking movies, 45–48, 118n31
technological determinism, 6, 17–19, 29, 40–42, 45, 105
technological essentialism, 40–45
technological progress, 105–6; Castoriadis on, 38–39, 42, 44–45; Gitelman on, 110n5
technology, 4, 33–49; ecology of, 28, 34, 41–42, 49, 117n22; historical logic of, 34–40; social conception of, 45–48; of writing, 44
technophilia, 7, 34, 44–48
technophobia, 7, 34, 44–45; silent movies and, 45–48, 118n31
temporal apparatus, 105, 106
terrorism, 2–3, 86, 94, 119n1
Thatcher, Margaret, 6, 16, 55
theodicy: democracy and, 57–60, 101; globalization and, 16, 110n5
Thoreau, Henry David, 95
Tocqueville, Alexis de, 57, 74, 125n76

topological capture, 4–5, 87, 104
torture, 23, 83, 99, 127n102
Tournier, Pierre, 36
"transformationalists," 24–25, 111n10
truth practices, 37, 80, 104
Tucker, Thomas Tudor, 73

unequal development, 1–2, 37, 39, 100, 109n2
USA PATRIOT Act, 23, 83, 85
U.S. Constitution: Bill of Rights, 84–86, 90–92; framing of, 70–72, 123n53, 127n108; on voting rights, 72, 92

Valéry, Paul, 51
value-concept, of democracy, 8, 51–57, 94, 101

Venezuela, 89, 98
Vico, Giambattista, 70
voter turnout, 89, 92
voting rights, 72, 92, 94, 119n4, 130n138. *See also* elections

Whig historiography, 59, 84–85, 93–94
Whitman, Walt, 75–76, 125n82
WikiLeaks, 83, 91, 118n35
Williams, Raymond, 41–42, 78, 115n52
Wilson, Woodrow, 81
Wolf, Martin, 22
Wolin, Sheldon, 59, 78, 81, 86, 88, 97–98
World Bank, 12

Zinn, Howard, 72

www.ingramcontent.com/pod-product-compliance
Lightning Source LLC
Chambersburg PA
CBHW051129160426
43195CB00014B/2406